MW00699200

They Knew Their God

Volume 1

E. & L. Harvey & E. Hey

BRITISH ADDRESS
Harvey Christian Publishers UK
P.O. Box 510, Cheadle
Stoke-on-Trent, ST10 2NQ
Tel./Fax (01538) 756391
E-mail: jjcook@mac.com

UNITED STATES ADDRESS
Harvey Christian Publishers, Inc.
3107 Hwy. 321 Hampton, TN 37658
Tel./Fax (423) 768-2297
E-mail: books@harveycp.com

Copyright 2003 by Harvey Christian Publishers
First Edition 1974
Sixth Edition 2009

Printed in USA

All rights reserved. No part of this book may be reproduced or trans-
mitted in any form or by any means, electronic or mechanical, including pho-
tocopying, recording, or by any information storage and retrieval system without written permission from the copyright owner, except for the inclusion of
brief quotations in a review.

Cover design by Vladmir Akhovich

Key to front cover—clockwise, beginning at bottom left corner: Alfred
Cookman, Lilias Trotter, Felix Neff, William Bramwell, Sister Eva, Christmas
Evans

ISBN 978-1-932774-09-2

Printed by
Old Paths Tract Society, Inc.
Shoals, Indiana 47581

Authors' Preface

"Walk about Zion . . . tell the towers thereof. Mark ye well her bulwarks, consider her palaces; that ye may tell it to the generation following." These words from the fortieth Psalm were impressed upon our minds nineteen years ago, as a commission to search into Christian biography and to pass on to the Lord's people that which had been so inspiring to us. And so after this lapse of time, we have the privilege of sending out these pictures of Zion's towers—her prophets and watchmen, Zion's bulwarks—her reformers and defenders of the faith, and Zion's palaces—those human dwellings of God, made beautiful and majestic by the presence of the King of kings.

The title, "They Knew Their God," has been chosen as one that includes the introduction to God via the New Birth, the receiving of the fullness of the Holy Spirit, and the further "journey into God," which progressively reveals His character. We have included characters from both sexes, from varying nationalities, from successive eras of time, and from differing church backgrounds.

God never repeats Himself in human experience, and it is refreshing to note that these saints, in venturing their all upon God, have left us individual histories which enrich the spiritual kingdom by that same delightful variety we discover in all God's "other" creations. We do not submit these sketches that they should be imitated in detail as to the individual's search for God, or as to his or her evidence of that attainment. We pray, rather, that the faith and courage of these saints in proving and knowing God, might encourage us to realize there is no limit, except in ourselves, to what we might discover of His kingdom while here in "time."

We have been most grateful for the collaboration of Miss Elizabeth M. Hey, a lifetime friend who has contributed much in biographical research and in writing and improving the text. Our daughter, Mrs. Gertrude Tait, has also improved some of these sketches and helped in completing others. We owe our grateful thanks for the secretarial assistance of our faithful helpers, Miss Beulah Freeman and the Misses Margaret and Morag Smith.

Daniel tells us that "the people that do know their God shall be strong and do exploits" (Dan. 11:32). It is our earnest prayer in this shallow, religious age, that these men and women who removed all barriers and boundaries to their search after and exploration of their own God in His length, breadth, depth and height, might beckon us on to a similar, unlimited grasp of the Unseen.

Edwin and Lillian Harvey, 1974

Publishers' Foreword

They Knew Their God, Volume One was first published in 1974 in the UK and, having been reproduced from the original many times, we thought it time to reset the book completely. Thanks to the voluntary labors of some good friends in Wisconsin to whom we are very grateful, the book was put on disc and then finally edited by us.

In our more recent publications, we cite the page and book from which each quotation has been taken. In the first edition of this book, this was not done, so we have gone to considerable pains to discover the sources for these quotations. When possible, we have listed these in the back under "Notes to Sources."

The last book in this series, *Volume Six*, was finished just weeks before my mother, Lillian Harvey, had several strokes which have incapacitated her for further writing and compiling. As she always gave me a "carte blanche" when it came to editing her manuscripts, I have taken the liberty, in her absence, to make minor changes to the text where improvement in punctuation etc. made this necessary. In checking the sources, sometimes adjustments in the text were necessary in order to ensure greater accuracy of quotation, or a sentence or two were added if there was space on the page. The poem at the end of the sketch on Robert Chapman was changed for one of his own, which we came across in recent years. And an editors' note was added after the chapter on Nicholas of Basle.

My husband and I now publish this new edition of *They Knew Their God, Volume One*, with thankfulness for the blessing it has been to so many over the years, and with the prayer that it may continue to challenge all of us to "Know our God" in a richer, fuller, and more abandoned way.

Trudy and Barry Tait, Hampton, 2003

Contents

NICHOLAS OF BASLE (1308 - 1398) 7
The Friend Of God

JOHN TAULER (1290 - 1361) 15
The Enlightened Doctor

CHRISTMAS EVANS (1766 - 1838) 25
One-eyed Preacher Of Wales

WILLIAM BRAMWELL (1754 - 1818) 39
Apostle Of Prayer

MOTHER COBB (1793 - ?) 47
Saint In Calico

FELIX NEFF (1798 - 1827) 55
The Brainerd Of The High Alps

ROBERT CLEAVER CHAPMAN (1803 - 1902) 68
The Rich, Poor Man

HOLY ANN (1810 - 1904) 76
The Irish Saint

ISAAC MARSDEN (1807 - 1882) 82
Earnest Merchant Preacher

ALFRED COOKMAN (1828   1871) 94
Washed In The Blood Of The Lamb

ELIZABETH BAXTER (1837 - 1926) 106
Christian "Heraldess"

LILIAS TROTTER (1853 - 1928) 117
The Frail Pioneer

JOHN HYDE (1865 - 1911) 127
The Praying Missionary

SAMUEL LOGAN BRENGLE (1860 - 1936) 135
Soldier And Servant

EVA VON WINKLER (1866 - 1932) 146
Mother Eva Of Friedenshort

SAMUEL MORRIS (1872 - 1893) 159
Angel In Ebony

IVA VENNARD (1871 - 1945) 171
Dedicated Educator

JOHANNA VEENSTRA (1894 - 1932) 184
A Flame For God

NOTES TO SOURCES 194

Nicholas of Basle

THE FRIEND OF GOD

Pope Gregory sat amazed! In agitation he looked at the two strangers from beyond the Alps. The leader, a man in his sixties, was addressing him in the Italian vernacular. His companion, when he spoke at all, used the language of learning—Latin. Both men were very much in earnest. Surely they must realize that many a man had been burned at the stake for saying less!

"Holy Father," began Nicholas, "the great and grievous sins of Christendom have risen to such a pitch, in all classes of men, that God is greatly displeased. You must consider what is to be done."

"I can do nothing," retorted the Pontiff, his anger increasing.

The older man was speaking again with the serenity and authority of one conveying a message from a higher source. God had shown him, he said, what an evil life the Pope was living. "Know of a truth that," he told the Pope, "if you do not turn from your evil ways and judge yourself before God, He will judge you, and you will die before the year is out."

The Pope was now enraged, but the speaker continued, "We are quite willing to be put to death, if the tokens which I am prepared to give you are not sufficient to prove that we are sent of God."

"What tokens, I should like to know?" demanded Gregory.

He calmed down quickly, as the account was given of what God had told this fearless man. So accurate was the listing of those sins, which no man could know except by revelation, that it convinced his hearer. The "Bishop of Rome" remained speechless for a while, and then he arose and embraced the two, speaking kindly for the first time. "Could you but give such tokens to the Emperor," he commented, "it would be well for Christendom."[1]

He asked them to remain in Rome that he might rely on them for counsel, promising to house them well. But they begged leave to depart, saying they would return at the Pope's request if they were needed at any time. He wrote a letter to the clergy in their area, commending these men of God to the formers' good offices. Unfortunately, this man in highest authority soon drifted from this temporary influence for good and forgot the effects of the meeting. He continued in his sins and died just within a year's time as had been predicted.

This fearless spokesman of God was Nicholas of Basle. To most people, however, he was known as the "Friend of God" from the Oberland (High Alps). What was his secret? How was he enabled, for over half a century, to spread the evangelical message under the very eyes of Rome?

He was born in the city of Basle in or about the year 1308. His father, a wealthy merchant, was called "Nicholas of the Golden Ring." The boy's prospects from a material point of view were bright indeed. However, at the age of thirteen, he went at Easter time to hear preaching on the sufferings and death of our Lord. The lad was profoundly moved and at once bought himself a crucifix. He knelt secretly every night, meditating on the pain and shame which our Lord suffered. It is surprising that, with his meager knowledge of spiritual things, his unusual honesty made him cry out for a revelation of God's will, whether he was to be a merchant or a priest. He asked for strength to be obedient. Somehow he obtained access to a Bible, whether it was his own or not, is not quite clear.

When he was fifteen, he began to travel with his father to learn the merchant's trade. Business and pleasure soon crowded out more serious thoughts. However, he never ceased to kneel nightly before his crucifix. He became a fast friend of the son of a knight, but the death of his father, four years later, necessitated a lengthy business journey for Nicholas. Upon his return, he found that his mother, too, had passed away.

He was now twenty-four years of age and wealthy. He and his young noble friend soon were engaged in a mad pursuit of pleasure, attending the tournaments and jousts, visiting courts and castles. They became popular, often entertaining "fair ladies" with songs and travelers' tales.

His friend soon married, but, although betrothed to a lady called Margaret, Nicholas was forced to wait because of her parents' opposition to her becoming the wife of a merchant. After six years this obstacle was overcome, and preparations were made for the festive occasion. But the eve of the wedding proved to be the turning point of Nicholas' life. It found him, not celebrating, but in his room, alone with his crucifix and absorbed in thoughts of a most serious nature. He writes:

> There was I all alone till the early morning, and I thought how vain and false was all the world could give me, and I thought of the bitter end of all the things of the world. And I said thus to myself, "Oh thou poor, unhappy man, how senseless hast thou been, that thou hast loved and chosen the things of time, rather than the things of eternity! Thou and all the men around thee, how foolish and senseless are you all, for, though God has given you richly your senses and your understanding, yet have you been dazzled with the glory and the pleasure that lasts but for a little while, and that gain for you at last an eternity in Hell."
>
> . . . And, kneeling before Him on my knees, I said, "Oh merciful God, I implore Thee now to have mercy upon me, a poor sinner, and to come to my help, for I must needs, with this evil heart of mine, take leave forever of this false and deceitful world and of all the creatures in it. And especially must I give up the one who is right dear to me, and to whom I have lost my heart."
>
> . . . And, when I had said this, I felt as though my whole nature gave way, for it was a terrible and solemn time of warfare against my own will and desires, so that the blood flowed from my mouth and nose, and I thought within myself the bitter hour of death was come. But I said to myself, "Oh nature, if it cannot be otherwise, even so it must be; if thou must die, thou must die."[2]

He then placed his left hand, which he said represented his sinful self, into his right one, which he felt stood for his "righteous and loving God" and vowed to be ever and always God's alone. After this, he had such a sense of the divine Presence that he could say, "I forgot myself and all creatures besides, and I was lost in joy and wonder, such as I can never tell, nor can the heart conceive it."[3] Nicholas added that he heard a "voice, very sweet," accepting him as His betrothed forever.

We can only imagine the storm that broke when the bridal party arrived the next morning. Relatives and guests were furious at the decision of the "madman." The bride to be was inconsolable until a few days later, when she and Nicholas were encouraged to meet briefly and he told her what had taken place. From that time, Margaret felt that she, too, must be wholly the Lord's, and the two never saw one another again. The outcome of this unusual situation shows, to the glory of God, what any man anywhere can be, as a channel of light and love, when he gives himself wholly to God.

We pass briefly over the next four years. This honest young man, with none to guide him, read the lives of the saints. As a result, he sought God by the only path that they could point out. He provided himself with a hair shirt, into which he fixed a number of sharp nails. He scourged himself till the blood ran down. He lived alone and was worn out with fastings and torments. At the end of a year, he cried to God in desperation and received an answer that these austerities had been born of self-will and of self-righteous pride. He was convinced by the Voice that seemed to speak to him, that he must throw away his instruments of self-imposed torture and that, as he sought and did God's will, He would bring all the necessary suffering into his life. The second year he spent in lamenting his sinfulness. The third year was one of fierce temptation. In the fourth he experienced, in addition, much of pain and sickness.

We cannot but wonder how different would have been the years between his spiritual awakening and the sense of divine acceptance and assurance, had there been available to him a teacher who knew God. But doubtless his heavenly Father used them to prepare Nicholas for a unique ministry to any, high or low, who would be seeking Him as he had done, endeavoring to establish his own righteousness by penance and good works.

At the end of this period, he suddenly emerged from the dark valley. His joy at the deliverance was so great that, fearing it was another temptation, he fell on his knees, telling God he wanted liberation and happiness, only if it were His will. Referring to this prayer, he said:

As I spake these words, there shone around me, as it were, a fair and blessed light, the light that is love, and from the glory of that light, a radiance filled my soul, so that whether I were in the body or out of the body I could not tell. For my eyes were opened to see the wonder and the beauty that are far above the mind of man, and I cannot speak thereof, for there are no words to tell it. . . As I was marveling thereat and rejoicing greatly, I heard, as it were, the gladdest and the sweetest Voice, which came not from myself, but yet it came to me as one who spake within me, but it was not my thoughts that it spake. And thus spake this inner and sweet Voice to me:

"Thou beloved and betrothed of My heart, now at last art thou verily My betrothed, and henceforth shalt thou ever be, and thou shalt know that as I have dealt with thee, so have I dealt with all My beloved friends, leading them by the way which thou has gone these four years past. And yet only now art thou at last in the true way, the way of love, receiving from Me the forgiveness of all thy sins, and knowing that there is no purgatory to come. For when thy soul shall pass from the earthly house, it will be to dwell with Me.

" . . . And so long as thou art in the earthly body, thou shalt not torment thyself with hard penances and chastisements, but shalt simply obey the commandments of Christ. And thou shalt find enough to suffer in this present evil world, if thou hast learnt to see that thy fellowmen are wandering as sheep amongst the wolves. And this shall move thy heart to depths of pity, and this shall henceforth be thy cross and thy suffering, and thou shalt be well exercised henceforth therewith."[4]

The Voice then said it would never again speak in the same way during Nicholas' lifetime, because it would not be needed.

In those parts of Switzerland and adjoining districts of France, the Waldenses had settled. Called so after Peter Waldo of Lyons, who lived about the year 1100, they were, however, found under different names in other lands. They claimed to trace their origin back to the fourth century, when the Church was forsaking the teachings of the early Christians and substituting for them the traditions of men. Learning the way of salvation by faith, they placed no dependence upon many practices adopted by the Church of Rome during the years. They encountered fierce persecution, thousands being burned at the stake or tortured in other ways. Those who fled for refuge to the higher cantons of Switzerland were known as the Vaudois.

In other parts, whole towns and even provinces were at times placed under an Interdict of the Pope—a terrible curse, which withdrew the consolations of absolution and forbade the regular ministry of the priesthood in preaching, burying the dead, and other ministries. In those dark times, such a penalty was dreadful indeed, because of the accumulated superstitions of years, as well as the absolute power of the papacy.

Those believers who proved, both by conduct and message, that they had a special relationship with their Lord, were called "Friends of God." In time, the name was used for all who were especially under the influence of Nicholas. This Spirit-filled, Heaven-directed man and his fellow-laborers ministered alike to those regarded as heretics and to any searching for God within the fold of the Church. Nicholas and four others, two of whom were priests and one a Jew converted through contact with him, built a home high up in the Alps. Its whereabouts was known only to a few. These five, with two servants, devoted themselves to lives of prayer in this hidden spot.

Nicholas was the acknowledged leader and, under his guidance, a ministry was established which searched out inquiring souls along the Rhine to Holland, into the lower cantons of Switzerland, in Alsace and Bavaria, and as far east as Hungary, as well as many other places.

Only occasionally did he himself travel afar, but sometimes this "Friend of God" would journey forth, teaching the way more perfectly. More frequently, however, he would send a letter by a messenger who would contact those who yearned to know the true message of salvation by faith, through the merits of Christ alone. One of his special missions was to John Tauler, the eloquent preacher of Strasburg. Gradually the teacher became the pupil, and the listener proved to be the one who would lead the Doctor into an experience of reality with God. How this came about is related in the sketch entitled "John Tauler."

And so Nicholas toiled on, evading by his seclusion and doubt-less also by God's protection, those who would have prematurely ended his powerful ministry, the fruits of which were many. A hea-then man received a letter from the "Oberland" that answered all his longing inquiries and was used of God to lead him savingly to Christ. A noble lady, called Frickin, who joined herself to the "Friends of God," said the blessedness of this fellowship was so great that she felt as if she had come out from "purgatory into paradise."

Eventually, however, the more than sixty years of blessed min-istry of this man of God drew to a close. One, Martin of Mayence, was burned at the stake in Cologne in 1393, accused of having been affected by the teachings of Nicholas of Basle. He declared that outward works deserved no merit before God. He regarded himself as freed from the authority of the Church and made no distinction between priests and laymen.

When the century had only a year or two to run and Nicholas was almost ninety years of age, the final test came. Two "Friends," James and John, were seized at Vienna and brought before the In-quisition. The former was probably the lawyer who had accompa-nied Nicholas to Rome, the latter, the converted Jew. Nicholas was also apprehended, but so wise had he been that his persecutors could not find sufficient evidence to convict him. They demanded that he renounce the condemned pair as heretics. This he refused to do, saying that the three of them would be separated only for a moment and then they would be together with the Lord forever.

And so it was. The flames soon consumed these three "Friends of God," but it was indeed a veritable "chariot of fire" that con-veyed them into the presence of Him Who had been so real and Whose Voice had been "so sweet" these many years.

There are plenty to follow our Lord halfway, but not the other half. They will give up possessions, friends and honors, but it touches them too closely to disown themselves.—*Meister Eckhart.*

Publishers' Note:

In our search for sources for this book, we have been reminded that Nicholas of Basle is indeed a shadowy character about whom we know very little for certain. Even Frances Bevan in her book, *The Three Friends of God,* from which the material for this chapter and the next is taken, states that her history of Nicholas of Basle "may yet be open to correction from further researches which are now being made by painstaking historians (p. vi). She continues: "His history is one which appears to us so full of contradictions and possibilities that it is difficult to separate that which is true from much that is either invented or told in allegorical fashion. . . . This Nicholas was a strange mixture of marvelous faith in God, devotedness to His service, love for souls, clear light upon many points on which Romanist Christians were utterly dark, abject superstition, credulity, and ignorance. (pp. 20-21)

It is not surprising, therefore, that if Frances Bevan had her doubts, more recent authors and scholars have been much less credulous than she. Through research we discovered that the stories in this chapter and in the one following on John Tauler, come mostly from papers found in the possession of a 14th century Strasburg banker, Rulman Merswin, after his death. Many of these texts claim to be by or about a "friend of God from the Oberland" named Nicholas. Some 19th century writers (Karl Schmidt's 1866 biography *Nikolaus von Basel,* for instance, which was followed by the above mentioned book by Frances Bevan) believed that this mysterious "Friend of God" was the same as Nicholas of Basle, but most today follow the opinion of the Catholic scholar, Heinrich Denifle, that this is impossible.

Nicholas of Basle was accused of belonging to a movement called the "Free Spirit," whose members allegedly taught that immoral acts were permitted to people who were full of the Spirit. He was burned at the stake at Vienna between 1393 and 1397 (as told in this book). There is no way to know for sure whether these charges are true, and most of our information about him (if he was not the "Friend of God from the Oberland") comes from the records of the Inquisition. The stories of his conversion, ministry, and visit to the Pope concern the "Friend of God," while the story of his death comes from the records of the Inquisition. If, therefore, he was indeed the Friend of God from the Oberland who was evidently orthodox in his beliefs, then it calls into question the accusations of the Inquisition.

In the next chapter, the story of the "Friend of God's" visit to the "Master" also comes from Merswin's papers. The "Master" is not named as Tauler in the original text, but since Tauler was an extremely important preacher in Strasburg at the time, and since Merswin was his disciple, it is highly likely that the story refers to Tauler.

It is with some reluctance that we have inserted this note as we are aware that Nicholas' story has brought blessing to our readers. However, when attempting to bring to light characters from the shadows of centuries as far removed from the present as the 14th, there are bound to be some unanswered questions regarding the details of their lives and ministry, and, having become aware of just how many do remain unanswered with regard to Nicholas of Basle, we share these with our readers. It is hoped, however, that the spirit of this sketch will remain fragrant with blessing to all who read it.

John Tauler

THE ENLIGHTENED DOCTOR

"Should I flee, or should I remain?" The question was one of utmost importance to Dr. Tauler. The head of Christendom, the Pope of Rome, had placed the city of Strasburg under the curse of the Church, called an Interdict. The Pope's quarrel was with the Emperor Lewis of Germany because he had protected Marsilius of Padua, Rector of the University of Paris, whose teachings regarding the authority of the Church and the sufficiency of the atonement of Christ had been pronounced heretical by the Holy See.

John Tauler had been born in Strasburg, in Alsace, in the year 1290. His father was probably Nicholas Tauler, a senator of that city and a man of considerable wealth. The young man entered the Dominican order of monks at the age of eighteen or thereabouts and soon afterwards went to Paris to study theology at the Dominican college of St. Jacques. Most of the "Schoolmen," as the teachers of that period were called, seem to have specialized in lofty philosophical themes in which young Tauler took little interest.

Tauler was a humble man and would not have admitted anything but respect and loyalty to the Church and its teachings. He was sincere and courageous and possessed a great love for the people. Unbounded also was their admiration of his exceptional ability in the pulpit. Somehow, even in the face of the Interdict, he could not give way to fear as did many other clergymen. Despite his lack of knowledge of the grace of God in its reality, he was no proverbial "hireling."

And so, to the relief of the populace, he remained in the city. The masses flocked to hear him, and their appreciation evolved into a pride that their beloved Strasburg should have so great a teacher. He was possessed of a great knowledge of the Bible and a sincere purpose to benefit his hearers in a practical way. Visitors came from some distance to hear him as his fame spread, but his theories of self-improvement proved completely inadequate for the reproduction of any grace in his audience. In the year 1340, the crowds were greater than ever, and Tauler yearned over them, as he attempted to teach them the way to Heaven.

It was no surprise, therefore, when one day he noticed in the audience a humble looking stranger, whose interest appeared to be intense. The speaker naturally concluded that the man was deriving much good from his discourse. However, if the thoughts of the one in the pew could have been read from the pulpit, there would have been small room for pride. For this man from Switzerland was thinking thus: "The master," (he was called this because of his extensive learning), "is a very gentle, loving, good-hearted man by nature. He has also a good understanding of the Holy Scriptures. But he is dark as to the light of grace, for he has never known it."[1]

The visitor was called Nicholas, thought by some to be Nicholas of Basle and often referred to as "The Friend of God from the Oberland." He was, indeed, a true apostle of that dark era. Told three times in a dream to go to Strasburg and hear Dr. Tauler preach, he was convinced that the voice of God was urging him to help this great teacher into Gospel light. He spent all available time in prayer and, after listening to five sermons, approached the master and desired, according to the practice of the Roman Catholic Church, to make confession to him. The latter agreed, and Nicholas did so for twelve weeks, after which he asked the Doctor to preach a sermon showing how a man could reach the highest spiritual life possible in this world of sin.

This Dr. Tauler finally did, delivering a practical and scriptural message of twenty-four main headings, upholding, from a human point of view, the pinnacle of Christian perfection. The sermon dealt with self-emptying, humility, the crucified life, inner victory, perfect love, and simplicity of motive. However, it was all theory obtained through diligent study of the Bible. Indeed, those who think of that period of time as the dark ages, would not believe that a clergyman of that day could have portrayed so clearly what God requires of all who desire to be wholly His.

But the sermon omitted two most important facts—the utter degeneracy of man, with his consequent inability in himself to attain to that standard, and faith in the merits of Christ's atonement as the one and only avenue to the blessed experience portrayed. Nicholas wrote the entire sermon from memory, later reading it to Tauler who, amazed at the intelligence and ability of the writer, urged him to remain in Strasburg and listen to future addresses.

Imagine the master's consternation and surprise when he heard the following from the lips of this meek stranger:

> You are a great scholar and have taught us a good lesson in this sermon. But you yourself do not live according to it. Yet you try to persuade me to stay here that you may preach me yet another sermon. Sir, I give you to understand that man's words have in many ways hindered me much more than they have helped me. And this is the reason: it often happened that, when I came away from the sermon, I brought certain false notions away with me, which I hardly got rid of in a long while with great toil. But if the highest Teacher of all truth comes to a man, he must be empty and quit of all else and hear His voice only. Know ye, that when this same Master cometh to me, He teaches me more in one hour than you or all the doctors from Adam to the judgment day will ever do.[2]

The master took this in good part, urging his guest to remain in Strasburg a while longer. Nicholas agreed to do so, if the Teacher would permit him to speak freely to him under the seal of confession. He then proceeded to teach the one who had thought to instruct him. He declared that the reason Tauler's sermons "killed and did not make alive" was that, in reality, his desires were not toward God, but instead directed to His creatures, and especially toward one (himself) whom he loved above measure. In consequence, he had no single heart toward God. Then, becoming even more direct, Nicholas continued:

> And therefore, I liken your heart to an unclean vessel. And when the pure, unmixed wine of godly doctrine passes through that vessel which is spoiled and covered with lees, it comes to pass that your teaching has no good savor and brings no grace to the hearts of those who hear you. And whereas I further said that you were still in darkness and had not the true light, this is also true, and it

may be seen hereby that so few receive the grace of the Holy Spirit through your teaching.

And whereas I said that you were a Pharisee, that is also true, but you are not one of the hypocritical Pharisees. You have, notwithstanding, this mark of the Pharisees, that you love and seek yourself in all things and not the glory of God. Now examine, dear sir, and see if you are not a Pharisee in the eyes of God. For know, dear Master, a man is a Pharisee in God's sight, according to what his heart is bent upon. And truly in the sight of God, there are many Pharisees.[3]

As these words were spoken, Tauler fell on Nicholas' neck and kissed him, saying:

A likeness has come into my mind. It has happened, as it did to the heathen woman at the well. For know, dear son, that thou hast laid bare all my faults before my eyes. Thou hast told me what I had hidden up within me, and specially that there is one creature upon whom my affections are set. But I tell thee, of a truth, I knew it not myself, nor do I believe that any human being in the world can know of it. Doubt not, dear son, that thou hast it from God.[4]

In further conversations, Tauler revealed to Nicholas the fact that to be called a Pharisee had hurt him deeply. But the humble servant of Christ faithfully showed him how he, too, like those teachers of old, placed burdens on others that he did not lift and, like them, he often "said and did not."

"Dear master, look at yourself," he continued. "Whether you touch these burdens and bear them in your life is known to God and also to yourself. But I confess that, as far as I can judge of your present condition, I would rather follow your words than your life. Only look at yourself and see if you are not a Pharisee in the eyes of God, though not one of those false, hypocritical Pharisees whose portion is in Hell fire."

The master replied, "I know not what to say. This I see plainly, that I am a sinner and am resolved to better my life, if I die for it. Dear son, I cannot wait longer. I beg of thee, simply for God's sake, to counsel me how I shall set about this work; and show me and teach me how I may attain to the highest perfection that a man may reach on earth."[5]

Nicholas then told the Master that if he really desired to know the ways of God, he would set him an "ABC" lesson. He knew only too well that the strong-willed Teacher or any other man could not attain to these commands by mere striving. His desire was that this final burst of self-effort would cause Tauler to catch such a glimpse of his own insufficiency and nothingness that he could be given a divine revelation of the way of salvation by faith alone.

After three weeks, Tauler, in despair, confessed that he had experienced great agony of soul and would be dishonest if he said he had learned even the first letter of the lesson assigned. But, after another period of similar length, he sent for Nicholas, saying, "Dear son, rejoice with me, for I think that, with God's help, I could say the first line."[6]

How happy Nicholas was, for as Tauler pleaded that he teach him further, it was evident that the "Master" was approaching the end of all self-effort. He then gave advice which he knew would spell death to all that the great preacher held dear. In short, it was to take the way of the Cross, which confronts every one who would follow Christ. He suggested that Tauler temporarily cease from preaching and other ministerial duties, concentrating on his search for God.

This, said Nicholas, would mean friends would turn against him. The audiences, which he had held spellbound, would leave him in disgust. And so it happened. For two desolate years, Tauler refused to preach or teach. The populace became angry, calling him a mad man. As a result, he was deprived of his livelihood and, during that period, to relieve the pangs of hunger, he was forced to sell some of his much-loved books. He became ill and, when his friend next saw him, he urged Tauler to take better care of the body which had been given him by God. Nicholas, however, was encouraged and, bidding the Master persevere, promised to come to him any time he was needed.

But our heavenly Father was watching and waiting to be gracious. The revelation from Himself was now not far away. It is significant that it was at the time of the celebration of the feast of St. Paul's conversion that the greatest event of Tauler's life took place.

The Doctor was convicted for his sinfulness of heart and, under the revelation, became so ill that he could only lie on his bed, pleading, "O merciful God, have mercy upon me, a poor sinner, for Thy boundless mercy's sake, for I am not worthy that the earth should bear me." And, as he lay there, weak and stricken with sorrow, he heard a Voice saying, "Trust in God and be at peace; and know that when He was on earth as a man, He made the sick, whom He healed in body, sound also in soul."[7]

So great was his reaction to this message that, for a time, reason seemed to reel. When he came to himself, he was possessed of a strange, new, inner strength, and divine truth which before had been dark to him was now clear as the day. He sent for Nicholas, who, observing him with joy, exclaimed:

> I tell you of a truth, that now, for the first time, your soul has been touched by the Most High. And know that the letter which has slain you, also maketh you alive again, for it has now reached your heart in the power of the Holy Ghost. Your teaching will now come from the Holy Ghost, which before came from the flesh. For you have now received the light of the Holy Spirit, by the grace of God. And the Scriptures which you already know will now be made clear to you, for you will have an insight that you never had before.[8]

And so it was. Tauler was a new creature, alive and vibrant with a message from Heaven. Nicholas gave him money with which to redeem his books and advised him to begin preaching again. The Master announced a service and the people came but, instead of sounding forth the Word, he could only stand and weep. The crowd which had come in eager anticipation waited, but there was no sermon that day. The one-time orator had no words to utter; his entire frame continued to shake with sobs. At length, they dispersed in anger, believing Dr. Tauler to be more unbalanced than ever.

But the great, inner change had come and, in view of the dire spiritual need everywhere, it was impossible for the Doctor to long remain silent about what had taken place. His reputation or his own interests now meant nothing to him.

He remembered the monks and nuns, with their sacrifice and self-inflicted penance, as well as their professed sanctity. As he thought of their gross sins and follies, he longed to reveal to them the secret of his deliverance. So, knowing that he had a message from God, he preached in front of the convent to an assembly of nuns and others. Taking as his text, "Behold, the bridegroom cometh; go ye out to meet him," he spoke of Christ as the Bridegroom of the soul, which was the relationship the sisters claimed regarding the Lord Jesus.

What a message it was! Considered in the light of what happened at the close of the sermon, it must have been devastatingly convicting. The Holy Spirit smote hearts right and left as the speaker described the state of the professed Bride of Christ, filthy with self-interest, love of the world, its praise and greed. It was a loving but penetrating discourse on what is in the heart of every human being, regardless of his calling. The message concluded with a picture of the Bridegroom giving Himself for the cleansing and sanctification of the Church. When he had finished, about forty inquirers remained for some time sitting in silence in the churchyard.

The Master began preaching to the masses again, and the action proved to be indeed well-timed, for soon the community was visited with pestilence and earthquakes. These were followed by the dreadful "Black Death," which resulted in the deaths of about 16,000 persons in Strasburg and 14,000 in Basle. For six years, Dr. Tauler gave out the light of the Gospel to the living and the dying. Is it not wonderful that this great preacher was filled with the Holy Spirit for such a time?

There are frequent instances in the biographies of godly Europeans during the ensuing centuries, where the seeker after the deeper spiritual life went far back to the dark, pre-Reformation days and read John Tauler's sermons with great avidity and blessing. Two excerpts from his lectures will show the extent to which this searcher after God had discovered some of the profoundest of secrets:

> Those who go into God's vineyard are truly noble and highly-favored men, who in deed and truth rise above all creature things in

God's vineyard, for they seek and love nothing but simply God in Himself. They neither look to pleasure, nor to any selfish end, nor to that which is a mere outflow from God, for their inner man is wholly plunged in God, and they have no end but the praise and glory of God, that His good pleasure alone may be fulfilled in and through them and in all creatures. Hence they are able to bear all things and to resign all things, for they receive all things as from God's hand, and offer up to Him again in simplicity of heart all that they have received from Him, and do not lay claim to any of His mercies.

They are like a river that flows out with every tide, and then again hastens back to its source. So do these men refer all their gifts back to the Source whence they proceed and flow back again unto it themselves likewise. For inasmuch as they carry all the gifts of God back into their divine fountain, and do not claim any ownership in them, either for pleasure or advantage, and do not purpose this nor that, but simply God alone. God must of necessity be their only refuge and stay, outward or inward.

The summary of another lecture on one of the Beatitudes is as follows:

"Blessed are the pure in heart for they shall see God." A pure heart is more precious in the sight of God than aught else on earth. A pure heart is a fair, fitly adorned chamber, the dwelling of the Holy Ghost, a golden temple of the Godhead, a sanctuary of the only-begotten Son, in which He worships the Heavenly Father, an altar of the grand, divine sacrifice, on which the Son is daily offered to the Heavenly Father.

A pure heart is the throne of the Supreme Judge, the seat and secret chamber of the Holy Trinity, a lamp bearing the Eternal Light, a secret council-chamber of the Divine Persons, a treasury of divine riches, a storehouse of divine sweetness, a panoply of eternal wisdom, a cell of divine solitude, the reward of all the life and suffering of Christ.

Now what is a pure heart? It is, as we have said before, a heart which finds its whole and only satisfaction in God, which relishes and desires nothing but God, whose thoughts and intents are ever occupied with God, to which all that is not of God is strange and jarring, which keeps itself as far as possible apart from all unworthy images, and joys and griefs, and all outward cares and anxieties, and makes all these work together for good, for to the pure all things are pure, and to the gentle is nothing bitter. Amen.

The godly life of John Tauler and his uncompromising teachings influenced two other men of the Church, Thomas of Strasburg and Ludolph of Saxony, both of whom were priors. These three "Friends of God," as they and others like them often were called, were fearless in their teachings and writings, which were startlingly in contrast with the tenets held by the Church in power. They counseled the people to take no heed to the Interdict of the Pope, to visit the sick and the dying, comforting them by pointing them to the "death and sufferings of our Lord, Who had offered up Himself as the perfect Sacrifice for them and for the sin of the whole world."

Vengeance on the part of their enemies was sure, and the three eventually were removed from their positions of influence. Six years after his conversion, Tauler was forced to leave Strasburg for Cologne, to the grief of many, not a few of whom had experienced changed lives during his ministry. In that city he was free to preach as he would, which he did for about ten years.

At seventy years of age, ill and infirm, he returned to Strasburg where he was nursed by his aged sister in one of the houses belonging to the convent in which she was a nun. There Nicholas visited him, and together they agreed that he should write an account of Tauler's life, though he was never to mention the Doctor by name. He was to be known only as "the Master" and Nicholas as "the man," that God might have all the glory from anything he had accomplished. Soon after this, the dear man of God went to be forever with the Lord. Nicholas and the townspeople mourned him deeply.

Martin Luther held the writings of Dr. Tauler in the highest esteem and declared that in them he had found more to instruct him than in those of all the schoolmen put together. To his friend, Spalatin, he wrote, "If you desire to make acquaintance with sound teaching of the good old sort in the German tongue, get John Tauler's sermons, for neither in Latin, nor in our own language, have I ever seen any teaching more solid or more in harmony with the Gospel."[9]

For many years, Tauler was remembered in Strasburg as "The Doctor who was enlightened by the grace of God," or "The Master of the Holy Scriptures."

WHAT THOU ART TO ME

As the bridegroom to his chosen,
　　As the king unto his realm,
As the keep unto the castle,
　　As the pilot to the helm,
　　　So, Lord, art Thou to me.

As the fountain in the garden,
　　As the candle in the dark,
As the treasure in the coffer,
　　As the manna in the ark,
　　　So, Lord, art Thou to me.

As the ruby in the setting,
　　As the honey in the comb,
As the light within the lantern,
　　As the father in the home,
　　　So, Lord, art Thou to me.

As the sunshine to the heavens,
　　As the image to the glass,
As the fruit unto the fig-tree,
　　As the dew unto the grass,
　　　So, Lord, art Thou to me.
　　　　　　　　　—John Tauler.

Christmas Evans

ONE-EYED PREACHER OF WALES

The newly converted lad of seventeen, with several friends, was trudging along a dark and lonely road in Wales to meet his pastor and study the Word of God. Suddenly, six youths armed with sticks sprang out from a place of concealment and ruthlessly attacked them. Christmas Evans was struck on his head in such a brutal fashion that he lost the vision in one eye. It seems that former companions, enraged at his complete abandonment of his former life of gross sin and drunkenness, had decided to trounce him in a way he would never forget. He was to be known in later years as the one-eyed preacher.

The early life of Christmas Evans gave no promise of his future as a minister of the glorious Gospel. He was born into the home of a poor shoemaker and his wife, Samuel and Johanna Evans, Christmas Day, 1766, in Cardiganshire, Wales. The father passed away when the child was eight, leaving the family in abject poverty. A maternal uncle offered to assume the care of his small nephew. In later years, Christmas said it "would be difficult to find a more unconscionable man than James Lewis in the whole course of a wicked world."[1] The lad was given no schooling in the six desperately unhappy years he spent with his drunken and cruel uncle and, until the age of seventeen, he could not read a word.

Christmas' life was miraculously preserved numerous times during adolescence. As an elderly man, he recounted the religious impressions of his youth:

> The fear of dying in an ungodly state especially affected me, even from childhood, and this apprehension clung to me till I was induced to rest upon Christ. All this was accompanied by some little knowledge of the Redeemer, and now, in my seventieth year, I cannot deny that this concern was the dawn of the day of grace on my spirit, although mingled with much darkness and ignorance.[2]

During a revival which took place in the church under the care of Mr. David Davies, many young people united themselves with that people, and I amongst them. . . .

One of the fruits of this awakening was the desire for religious knowledge that fell upon us. Scarcely one person out of ten could, at this time and in those neighborhoods, read at all, even in the language of the country. We bought Bibles and candles and were accustomed to meet together in the evening, in the barn of Penyralltfawr, and thus, in about one month, I was able to read the Bible in my mother tongue. I was vastly delighted with so much learning.

This, however, did not satisfy me, but I borrowed books and learnt a little English. Mr. Davies, my pastor, understood that I thirsted for knowledge and took me to his school, where I stayed for six months. Here I went through the Latin Grammar, but so low were my circumstances that I could stay there no longer.[3]

The night after the impairment of his sight, he had a singular dream. He seemed to see the world aflame, with its inhabitants summoned to final judgment. The cry, "Jesus, save me!" leaped to his lips, and the Son of God turned to him saying, "It was thy intention to preach the Gospel, but now it is too late, for the Judgment Day has come." The impression made was so vivid that the young man purposed to enter the ministry.

Cottage meetings were much in vogue in Wales, and Christmas, in his ardent desire to proclaim the message of salvation that had reached his sinful heart, borrowed a book from his pastor and memorized one of the sermons it contained. He also learned a prayer. Both his address and petition in a private home bid fair to establish his reputation as a preacher, until it was discovered that his words were those of others.

The church with which Christmas was affiliated was Presbyterian, though united with one of the Unitarian faith. But the young man, now twenty-three years of age and possessed of a growing desire to please God, was attracted to the more evangelical Baptist persuasion.

The call to Gospel ministry was "as burning fire" shut up in his bones, but since his memorized message had proved a failure, upon his next attempt he selected a text at random and discoursed with no previous preparation. "If it was bad before, it was worse now," was his analysis of the result. "So I thought God would have nothing to do with me as a preacher."[4]

However, through such humiliating experiences, God prepared His servant for future usefulness. Of this most difficult period, Christmas wrote:

> I was filled with most depreciatory thoughts of myself. I was brought soon to preach in company with other preachers, and I found them altogether better and godlier preachers than I was; I could feel no influence, no virtue in my own sermons. . . . I traveled much in this condition, thinking every preacher a true preacher but myself, nor had I any confidence in the light I had upon Scripture. I have since seen God's goodness in all this, for thus was I kept from falling in love with my own gifts, which has happened to many young men and has been their ruin.

His superiors had taken notice of his ability and, after ordaining him, offered him the pastorate of a church in Lleyn, a small village on Caernarvon Bay—the most discouraging place the Baptists had in Wales. Here he waited upon God for a deeper Christian life and the Holy Spirit came upon him with power. Confidence in prayer, a care for the cause of Christ, and a new revelation of the plan of salvation were the results. In his humility, he seemed utterly unaware of the effect of his ministry upon the parish.

> I could scarcely believe the testimony of the people who came before the Church as candidates for membership, that they were converted through my ministry, yet I was obliged to believe, though it was marvelous in my eyes. This made me thankful to God and increased my confidence in prayer. A delightful gale descended upon me as from the hill of the New Jerusalem, and I felt the three great things of the kingdom of Heaven, "righteousness, and peace, and joy in the Holy Ghost."[5]

The whole area, hitherto so dead and impervious to anything spiritual, was marvelously revived.

At the beginning of his two-year ministry at Lleyn, he married a devoutly spiritual young woman, Catherine Jones. She had a very real sense of her acceptance with Christ and a keen perception of character and reality. Hardship and poverty never daunted her, and out of her penury much was freely given to many needy ones about her. Catherine accompanied her husband on five of his arduous journeys across Wales.

Christmas Evans often preached five times on the Sabbath, walking a distance of twenty miles to reach the scattered appointments. Before leaving Lleyn, he visited South Wales where he established a reputation for being the most outstanding preacher in the Principality, and was henceforth a much sought-after minister. It was there at an annual conference of the Association when all nonconformists met for business purposes, that services were also conducted for the local inhabitants. Sometimes the assembled congregations numbered as many as 15,000.

At Felinfoel, two well-known ministers were to preach, but they were late in coming. "Why not ask that one-eyed lad from the North? I heard that he speaks quite wonderfully," someone suggested, and Evans, "a tall, bony, haggard young man, uncouth and ill-dressed," consented.[6] As he took his stand in the pulpit, judging from his appearance, many thought a sad mistake had been made and decided to relax in the shade of the hedges or to partake of the refreshments they had brought until the appointees arrived. His biographer writes:

> He took a grand text: "And you, that were sometimes alienated and enemies in your mind by wicked works, yet now hath he reconciled in the body of his flesh through death, to present you holy and unblamable and unreproveable in his sight." Old men used to describe afterwards how he justified their first fears by his stiff, awkward movements, but the organ was, in those first moments, building, and soon it began to play. He showed himself a master of the instrument of speech.
>
> Closer and closer the audience began to gather near him. They got up and came in from the hedges. The crowd grew more and more dense with eager listeners; the sermon became alive with dramatic representation. The throng of preachers present confessed

that they were dazzled with the brilliance of the language and the imagery, falling from the lips of this altogether unknown and unexpected young prophet.

Presently, beneath some appalling stroke of words, numbers started to their feet, and in the pauses—if pauses were permitted in the paragraphs—the question went, "Who is this? Whom have we here?". . . . The people began to cry, "Gogoniant!" (Glory!) "Bendigedig!" (Blessed!). The excitement was at its highest when, amidst the weeping and rejoicing of the mighty multitude, the preacher came to an end.[7]

Christmas Evans returned to Lleyn full of joy, but feeling that Providence was indicating labor elsewhere. He observed:

> I must now refer to my departure from Caernarvonshire. I thought I saw symptoms of the Divine displeasure on the Baptists there. Three things have borne down our interest: the want of practical godliness in some of the preachers that have been there; the absence of an humble and evangelical taste in the ministry, and the prominence of a sour condemnatory temper, burning up everything, like the scorching heat of summer, until not a green blade is to be seen; and, lastly, serious defects of character, both as to mind and heart, in many of the leading members.

When invited to superintend the Baptist churches on the island of Anglesey, he complied, receiving the promise of a salary of seventeen pounds a year. He and his young wife rode to the new appointment on horseback. They settled at Llangefni where a small cottage which had fallen into disuse was their only accommodation. The stable joined the house. The ceiling was so low that Christmas was forced to use caution when standing. The furniture was scanty. But in this humble place, some of his most powerful and eloquent sermons were born.

The pinch of poverty was felt to such an extent that Mr. Evans was obliged to occasionally print small pamphlets, selling them from door to door. He writes:

> It pleased God to bring two benefits out of my poverty: one was the extension of my ministry, so that I became almost as well

known in one part of the Principality as the other; and secondly, he gave me the favor and the honor to be the instrument of bringing many to Christ, through all the counties of Wales, from Presteign to St. David's, and from Cardiff to Holyhead. Who will speak against a preacher's poverty, when it thus spurs him to labor in the vineyard?

During the first part of his ministry in Anglesey, the Baptist societies became involved and almost engulfed in the Sandemanian controversy. Its leader, a brilliant man by the name of John Richard Jones, adopted certain practices of the primitive Christian Church in his services, such as the kiss of charity, the feast of love, and foot washing. He severely criticized all religious bodies, enjoining such a complete separation from them that both he and his adherents became extremely uncharitable and indifferent to the needs of humanity at large. His following, though numbering only about 200 persons, caused great distress and dissension. Evans agreed with some aspects of the controversy but, in his zeal to refute the wrong, gave way to ill-feeling and bitterness. In regard to this, he confessed:

> The Sandemanian heresy affected me so far as to quench the spirit of prayer for the conversion of sinners, and it induced in my mind a greater regard for the smaller things of the kingdom of Heaven, than for the greater. I lost the strength which clothed my mind with zeal, confidence, and earnestness in the pulpit for the conversion of souls to Christ. My heart retrograded in a manner, and I could not realize the testimony of a good conscience.
>
> Sabbath nights, after having been in the day exposing and vilifying, with all bitterness, the errors that prevailed, my conscience felt as if displeased and reproached me that I had lost nearness to, and walking with God. It would intimate that something exceedingly precious was now wanting in me. I would reply that I was acting in obedience to the Word, but it continued to accuse me of the want of some precious article. I had been robbed, to a great degree, of the spirit of prayer and of the spirit of preaching.[8]

The backbone of the heresy was broken when, in strong faith and in the power of the Holy Spirit, a certain minister, Thomas Jones, in a sermon at the Association of Baptists in 1802, dared to assail the arguments of the Sandemanians. "The religious ice-plant, religion in an ice house," was dealt with in the light of Scripture, and revival came to Wales and to Christmas Evans.

His confrontation with God, which turned the captivity of his soul "as the streams in the south," was described in a vivid way:

> I was weary of a cold heart towards Christ and His sacrifice and the work of His Spirit—of a cold heart in the pulpit, in secret prayer, and in the study. For fifteen years previously, I had felt my heart burning within, as if going to Emmaus with Jesus.
>
> On a day ever to be remembered by me, as I was going from Dolgelly to Machynlleth and climbing up towards Cader Idris, I considered it to be incumbent upon me to pray, however hard I felt in my heart, and however worldly the frame of my spirit was. Having begun in the name of Jesus, I soon felt, as it were, the fetters loosening, and the old hardness of heart softening, and, as I thought, mountains of frost and snow dissolving and melting within me.
>
> This engendered confidence in my soul in the promise of the Holy Ghost. I felt my whole mind relieved from some great bondage; tears flowed copiously, and I was constrained to cry out for the gracious visits of God, by restoring to my soul the joys of His salvation, and that He would visit the churches in Anglesey that were under my care. I embraced in my supplications all the churches of the saints and nearly all the ministers in the Principality by their names.
>
> This struggle lasted for three hours; it rose again and again, like one wave after another, on a high flowing tide, driven by a strong wind, until my nature became faint by weeping and crying. Thus I resigned myself to Christ, body and soul, gifts and labors—all my life—every day and every hour that remained for me, and all my cares I committed to Christ. The road was mountainous and lonely, and I was wholly alone and suffered no interruption in my wrestlings with God.
>
> From this time, I was made to expect the goodness of God to churches and to myself. Thus the Lord delivered me and the people of Anglesey from being carried away by the flood of Sandemanianism. In the first religious meetings after this, I felt as if I had been removed from the cold and sterile regions of spiritual frost, into the verdant fields of divine promises. The former striving with God in prayer and the longing anxiety for the conversion

of sinners which I had experienced at Lleyn were now restored. I had a hold of the promises of God. The result was when I returned home, the first thing that arrested my attention was that the Spirit was working also in the brethren in Anglesey, inducing in them a spirit of prayer.[9]

At this period "under a deep sense of the evil of his own heart and in dependence upon the infinite grace and merit of the Redeemer," he made a solemn covenant with God which reads as follows:

1. Jesus, I give my soul and body unto Thee, the true God, and everlasting life. Bring me into everlasting life. Amen.

2. I call the day, the sun, the earth, the trees, the stones, the bed, the table, and the books, to witness that I come unto Thee, Redeemer of sinners, that I may obtain rest for my soul from the thunders of guilt and the dread of eternity. Amen.

3. Through confidence in Thy power, I do earnestly entreat Thee to take the work into Thine own hands. Give me a circumcised heart so that I may love Thee. Create in me a right spirit that I may seek Thy glory. Grant me that principle which Thou wilt own in the day of judgment so that I may not then assume pale-facedness and find myself a hypocrite. Grant me this for the sake of Thy most precious blood. Amen.

4. Jesus, Son of God, I entreat Thee in power to grant me, for the sake of Thy agonizing death, a covenant interest in Thy blood which cleanseth, in Thy righteousness which justifieth, and in Thy redemption which delivereth. I entreat an interest in Thy blood for Thy blood's sake, and a part in Thee for Thy name's sake, which name Thou has given among men. Amen.

5. O Jesus Christ, Son of the living God, take, for the sake of Thy cruel death, my time and my strength and also the gifts and talents I possess. These, with a full purpose of heart, I consecrate to Thy glory in the building up of Thy Church in the world—for Thou art worthy of the hearts and talents of men. Amen.

6. My great High Priest, I desire Thee from Thy High Court and by Thy power to confirm my usefulness as a preacher and my piety as a Christian—as two gardens nigh to each other—so that sin may not have place in my heart to becloud my confidence in Thy righteousness, and so that I may not be left to any foolish act that

may occasion to wither my gifts, and I be rendered useless before my life ends. O my Lord and my God, keep Thy gracious eye upon me and watch over me forever! Amen.

7. O Jesus Christ the Savior, I give myself in a particular manner to Thee to be preserved from the falls into which many stumble, that Thy name (in Thy cause) may not be blasphemed or wounded, so that my peace may not be injured, and Thy people not be grieved, and Thine enemies not be hardened. Amen.

8. I come entreating Thee to enter into a covenant with me in my ministry. Oh prosper me as Thou didst prosper Bunyan, Vavasor, Powell, Howell, Harris, Rowlands, and Whitefield. The impediments in the way of my prosperity remove. That I may attain this, work in me the things approved of God. Give me a heart "sick of love" to Thyself, and to the souls of men. Grant that I may feel the power of Thy Word before preaching it, as Moses felt the power of his rod before he saw it on the land and waters of Egypt. Jesus, my All in all, grant me this for the sake of Thy precious blood. Amen.

9. Search me now, and lead me into plain paths of judgement. May I in this world see what I really am in Thy sight so that I may not find myself otherwise when the light of eternity shall dawn upon me and when I open my eyes in the brightness of immortality. Wash me in Thy redeeming blood. Amen

10. Give me power to trust in Thee for food and raiment and to make known my requests to Thee. Oh let Thy care be over me as a covenant privilege betwixt Thee and me—not simply as the general care to feed the ravens that perish, and in clothing the lily that is cast into the oven, but remember me as one of Thy family and as one of Thy unworthy brethren. Amen.

11. O Jesus, take upon Thyself to prepare me for death, for Thou art God and needest but to speak the word. Thy will be done, but if possible, let me not linger in sickness nor die a sudden death without bidding adieu to my brethren, but rather, after a short illness, let me die with them around me. May everything be put in order for that day of passing from one world to another so that there be no confusion nor disorder, but a passing away in peace. O grant me this for the sake of Thine agony in the garden. Amen.

12. O blessed Lord, grant that no sin may be nourished or fostered in me which may cause Thee to cast me off from the work of Thy sanctuary like the sons of Eli. For the sake of Thine infinite merits, let not my days be longer than my usefulness. Let me not

become at the end of my days like a piece of lumber that is in the way of the usefulness of others. Amen.

13. My Redeemer, I beseech Thee to present these supplications of mine before the Father. While I am writing them on earth with my mortal hand in my book, oh inscribe them in Thy book with Thine own immortal pen. According to the depths of Thy merit, Thine infinite grace, Thy compassion, and Thy tenderness toward Thy people in Thy Upper Court attach Thy name to these humble supplications of mine. Set Thine Amen to them, even as I set mine on my side of the covenant. Amen.—Christmas Evans, Llangefni, Anglesey, April 10.[10]

Then he added, from a heart overflowing with love to God, "I felt a sweet peace and tranquillity of soul, like unto a poor man that had been brought under the protection of the Royal Family and had an annual settlement for life made upon him, and from whose dwelling painful dread of poverty and want had been forever banished away."[11]

What has been called the "Graveyard Sermon" established Evans' reputation for all time to come. The "one-eyed man of Anglesey," in a small dell amid the mountains of Caernarvonshire, stood "six feet high, his face very expressive, but very calm and quiet," according to his biographer. "But a great fire was burning within the man. He gave out some verses of a well-known Welsh hymn and, while it was being sung, took out a small phial from his waistcoat pocket, wetting the tips of his fingers and drawing them over his blind eye. It was laudanum, used to deaden the excruciating pain which, upon some occasions, possessed him."

His text was Romans 5:15: "If through the offense of one many be dead, much more the grace of God, and the gift by grace, which is by one man, Jesus Christ, hath abounded unto many." He pictured the world as an immense graveyard, surrounded by massive walls which enclosed the dying race of Adam. This sermon, translated into English, has become a veritable classic. Only a man who had spent much time in God's presence could have obtained such a conception of the fall and redemption of mankind and delivered such a message.

Christmas' other sermons were as imaginative and as powerful. But, aside from the natural eloquence that captured the hearts of the hearers, those who listened never were the same again. So certain was the preacher himself of the fact that eternal realities supersede those of time that he was able to transfer his convictions to others. He remarked once to a brother minister, "The doctrine, the confidence and strength I feel will make people dance for joy in some parts of Wales."

In his ministry in Anglesey, Evans encountered unforeseen difficulties. Under his Spirit-inspired messages, congregations increased, with the resultant need of more chapels. And it was his responsibility to secure funds with which to build them. This meant travel by horseback for many miles throughout South Wales to seek the aid of more affluent churches. At one time, threatened with legal prosecution because of some chapel debts, he described his reaction to the injustice:

> They talk of casting me into a court of law, where I have never been, and I hope I shall never go, but I will cast them, first, into the court of Jesus Christ. . . . I knew there was no ground of action, but, still, I was much disturbed, being at the time sixty years of age and, having very recently buried my wife . . . I received the letter at a monthly meeting, at one of the contests with spiritual wickedness in high places. On my return home, I had fellowship with God, during the whole journey of ten miles and, arriving at my own house, I went upstairs to my own chamber and poured forth my heart before the Redeemer, Who has in His hands all authority and power.
>
> . . . I was about ten minutes in prayer. I felt some confidence that Jesus heard. I went up again with a tender heart; I could not refrain from weeping with the joy of hope that the Lord was drawing near to me. After the seventh struggle, I came down, fully believing that the Redeemer had taken my cause into His hands and that He would arrange and manage for me. My countenance was cheerful as I came down the last time, like Naaman, having washed himself seven times in the Jordan, or Bunyan's Pilgrim, having cast his burden at the foot of the cross into the grave of Jesus.
>
> I well remember the place—the little house adjoining the meeting house at Cildwrn. I can call it Penuel. No weapon intended

against me prospered, and I had peace, at once, to my mind and in my temporal condition. I have frequently prayed for those who would injure me that they might be blessed, even as I have been blessed. I know not what would have become of me, had it not been for these furnaces in which I have been tried, and in which the spirit of prayer has been excited and exercised in me.[12]

A series of trials assailed this devoted servant of God at this time. His wife and partner in tribulation was removed by death, and he was threatened by total blindness because of an illness which developed on a journey to the south and which kept him in Aberystwyth for some months under medical care. At one time, there seemed little hope of retaining the sight of his one remaining eye. But through faith and patience, he was brought through to the glory of God and the advancement of His kingdom.

Misunderstandings among ministers, jealous of his influence and success, brought about the removal from Anglesey of this remarkable man. Younger pastors desired independence and advancement. "Heresy," that convenient weapon, became the cry when many thought the old orator was departing from their Calvinistic heritage. Doubtless he had adopted a less extreme view as he had obtained further revelations of the grandeur of the atonement and of the scope of redemption. However, the basest of all instruments used to disparage this dear saint, was an accusation founded on a false report of an action performed thirty-four years previously. It is now apparent that Satan, whose kingdom Christmas Evans shook by the power of his ministry, was angry. But God doubtless used it to release him to preach the Gospel in other parts of Wales, and he is able to give us this joyous testimony:

> Nothing could preserve me in cheerfulness and confidence under these afflictions but the assurance of the faithfulness of Christ. I felt assured that I had much work yet to do and that my ministry would be instrumental in bringing many sinners to God. This arose from my trust in God and in the spirit of prayer that possessed me.
> . . . As soon as I went into the pulpit during this period, I forgot my troubles and found my mountain strong. I was blessed with such heavenly unction and longed so intensely for the salva-

tion of men, and I felt the truth like a hammer in power, and the doctrine distilling like the honeycomb, and like unto the rarest wine, that I became most anxious that the ministers of the country should unite with me to plead the promise, "If two of you shall agree on earth as touching any thing that they shall ask, it shall be done for them of my Father which is in heaven."[13]

At sixty-two years of age, he left Anglesey in 1828 to accept the charge of a poor little church in Caerphilly. The enthusiasm of his welcome did much to alleviate any distress of mind at the change. The words, "Christmas Evans has come," flew from cottage to cottage in the district. Many asked incredulously, "Are you sure?" "Yes, quite sure," would come the reply. "He preached at Caerphilly last Sunday." Here, it is said, the eloquence and power of his sermons surpassed those of all previous efforts, and every Sabbath the wild hills of Wales witnessed eager men and women making their way to the chapel.

He spent brief periods at Caerphilly and Cardiff, and then moved to Caernarvon, which proved to be his last pastorate. The church consisted of only thirty members of the lowest class, with those few quarrelling among themselves. In addition, a debt of £800.00, half of which Evans was expected to lift, hung over the place. Although Christmas was seventy years of age and so frail he feared he should die on the way, he set out to do his duty with his second wife, Mary, and a young preacher.

The purpose of his mission was accomplished, but the effort required more physical energy than he possessed. His final message was at Swansea where, as he descended the pulpit stairs, those around heard him say, "This is my last sermon." And it was. Through the following week, he suffered intermittently from physical exhaustion. Friday, July 19, 1838, he called his friends to his bedside. "I am leaving you," he told them. "I have labored in the sanctuary for fifty-three years, and my comfort is that I have never labored without blood in the basin," probably meaning he had not failed to preach a crucified Savior. "Preach Christ to the people, brethren," he continued. "Look at me. In myself I am nothing but ruin, but in Christ I am Heaven and salvation." Then, repeating a stanza from a favorite Welsh hymn and waving his hand, he sank back on the pillows with the words, "Good-bye! Drive on!" "His friends tried to rouse him," writes his biographer, "but the angelic postman had obeyed the order—the chariot had passed over the everlasting hills.[14]

I CONSECRATE

I consecrate my life to Thee, dear Lord;
To labor with my might, call nothing hard;
Use all my strength with every passing day,
Then ask for more, and hasten on my way;
Pluck brands from out the burning while I live,
Then Heavenward fall, and falling, Heaven receive.

I consecrate my powers of soul and mind;
In Thee my powers shall meet employment find.
My judgment and my will and memory store,
Imaginations, thoughts shall evermore
Be captive to my Christ, the crucified.
Each all its work perform, yet in Thee hide;
Affection's wealth, pour incense on Thy head,
And grosser appetites forever dead.

I consecrate my home, my friends, my all,
And forth I go, heeding Thy gracious call,
Ready for any place, afar or near—
The place that others shun I will not fear,
But gladly go, if I may only bring
One wanderer more, to serve my God and King.

I consecrate to do, to go, to dare,
To suffer with my Savior, and to bear
Hardness, as soldiers should, on every field—
To run the race, to weakness never yield;
Refuse all honor, ease or earthly store;
Take up the cross, deny self more and more;
Bend all my energies to save the lost,
And with some stars, gain Heaven at any cost.

—*Vivian A. Dake*

William Bramwell

APOSTLE OF PRAYER

An earnest Christian young woman was about to sail from Liverpool to visit friends living in Jamaica. It was in the days of the old sailing ships. The voyage would be long and fraught with perils. She decided to visit Rev. William Bramwell, a much esteemed Methodist minister in the city, and to ask him to commend her to God's blessing and protection. He received her graciously and then prayed fervently on her behalf.

When he arose from his knees, he exclaimed emphatically, "My dear sister, you must not go tomorrow. God has just told me you must not go." She was surprised, disappointed, and certainly confused, because her plans had all been made. However, she dared not ignore the warning of the man she knew to be in close touch with God. So, inconvenient though it was, she allowed him to accompany her to the ship and remove her luggage.

"The secret of the Lord is with them that fear him." God's servant had dwelt too constantly in the Lord's presence to miss the divine directive. Six weeks later, word reached England that the ship with all on board had been lost.

William Bramwell was born in February, 1759, in the village of Elswick, near Preston, Lancashire. He was a member of a large family. His parents were staunch adherents of the Church of England and attempted to rear their children in accordance with a strict code of morality.

A love for truth manifested itself in William after he had become an apprentice to a currier at the age of fifteen. Asked by his employer to confirm to a prospective customer the worth of a certain item, the boy spoke out bluntly, "No, Sir, the quality of that leather is not so good as you have represented it."[1] How the boss reacted we are not told, but this and other similar incidents being circulated, the lad gained quite a reputation for truthfulness.

But such a standing before men could not bring peace to his heart. He was a sinner, and he knew it only too well. He was a sober-minded young man and by faithful church attendance and good works endeavored to earn his salvation. Hatred for immorality pressed the youth to enter into the public houses to persuade some of the most degraded men to leave their lives of vice. But within his heart the tempest raged, as evil tempers and memories of past sins continually harassed him. He would resort to bodily austerities, such as kneeling with bare knees on sand, which somewhat remind us of the monks of the Dark Ages.

For a time, he attempted to embrace Roman Catholicism, but soon returned to the Church of his fathers. He spent hours in the attitude and posture of prayer, being especially devout before receiving the sacrament. God saw his hunger and, while the ceremony was being performed, his soul-cry was answered. In a moment, the way of salvation by faith in Christ opened up to him, and he found pardon and peace.

Having no spiritual instructor and being ignorant of Satan's devices, young Bramwell joined a group of church singers. These were merely nominal Christians and even met in a large room in a public house. Here frivolity and worldly entertainment soon had its deadening effect upon the young convert. He lost the comfort of the sense of sins forgiven.

Urged by a young Methodist preacher to attend services held by that "sect," he flatly refused. He had heard nothing but ill of them, and his father considered them deceivers and wolves in sheep's clothing. But later, hearing a Catholic woman defaming the Methodists, it dawned upon William that these were true followers of the despised Master and that the opposition of Satan and the world only proved their genuineness.

Just a few humble people assembled at the first service he attended. His heart was warmed. He said of the sermon, "Oh, this is the preaching I have long wanted to hear. These are the people with whom I am resolved to live and die."[2]

Soon after, the little band was visited by their founder, John Wesley. That night, Mr. Bramwell again found the comfort he had lost, and from that time was enabled to walk continually in the light of God's countenance. But he strongly felt the need of a deeper work within his heart. His very activities and much time spent in the presence of a holy God revealed to him the corruption of his natural heart.

How he sought and found the victory for which he longed is best told by himself:

> I was for sometime convinced of my need of purity and sought it carefully with tears, entreaties, and sacrifice, thinking nothing too much to do or suffer, if I might but attain this pearl of great price. Yet I found it not, nor knew the reason why, till the Lord showed me I had erred in the way of seeking it.[3]

> I did not seek it "by faith alone" but, as it were, by "the works of the law." Being now convinced of my error, I sought the blessing by faith only. Still it tarried a little, but I waited for it in the way of faith. When in the house of a friend at Liverpool, while I was sitting with my mind engaged in various meditations concerning my affairs and future prospects, my heart now and then lifted up to God, but not particularly about this blessing, Heaven came down to my soul. The Lord for Whom I had waited, came suddenly to the temple of my heart, and I had an immediate evidence that this was the blessing I had for some time been seeking. My soul was then all wonder, love and praise.[4]

During a fifteen-mile walk to a preaching appointment that night, the enemy whispered all the way, "Do not profess sanctification, for thou shalt lose it."[5] But the Lord won and, during his message, Bramwell told boldly and to the glory of God what great things had been done for his soul.

This was the commencement of one of the most fragrant walks with God we read of anywhere. Stripped of all self-confidence, Bramwell realized that there was no holiness apart from a life of constant communion with his heavenly Father. Two great passions literally consumed him. The first was to be in God's presence continuously. "I am giving myself to prayer," he emphasized over and over in his letters and journals.

Along with this deep love for God's presence, came a great longing for the salvation of the lost. Prayer, prayer, and more prayer was followed by intense labor for the souls of men in many of the large circuits in Northern England. Sleep, food, health—all were sacrificed to these two great loves.

When he was twenty-eight years of age, Mr. Bramwell married Miss E. Byrom. We know little of his family life, but at least two children, a son and a daughter, blessed the union. His letters to his daughter, Ann, are full of fatherly love and admonition.

His first appointment was to Blackburn, then Colne, and on to Dewsbury. Of his service in and about Dewsbury, Yorkshire, his biographer tells us:

> He gave himself to continual prayer for the outpouring of the Holy Spirit and was instant in season, out of season. In this work, he sought the cooperation of all who would unite with him and appointed prayer meetings at five o'clock in the morning. Such efforts could not be in vain.[6]

Mr. Bramwell remarks:

> As I was praying in my room, I received an answer from God in a particular way and had the revival discovered to me in its manner and effects. I had no more doubt. All my grief was gone. I could say, "The Lord will come. I know He will come and that suddenly." And, indeed, that is exactly what did happen very soon.[7]

After two weeks of visiting the various societies in the Sheffield circuit, he wrote:

> After diligent search, I have not found one person that knows the virtue of Christ's all-cleansing blood. Yet there is a great friendship, and it appears I am received by the people with much respect. I have seen nearly twenty set at liberty. I believe I should have seen many more, but I cannot find one pleading man. There are many good people, but I have found no wrestlers with God.
>
> Oh pray that I may see His arm laid bare in this place! . . . After twelve hours groaning and using every means, God has opened blind eyes. I never saw the power of God more visibly displayed.[8]

Twelve hundred and fifty members were added to the Society in the course of his first year's labor in this circuit. Removing to Nottingham, this man of prayer wrote:

> I am all weakness; indeed, I see nothing will do but a continual dependence and a living upon His mercy—and oh, the depth of mercy! It is continual prayer that brings the soul into all the glory.[9]

> I am striving with continual prayer to live nearer to God than I have ever done, and He brings my soul into closer union. I live with Jesus; He is my all. I am less than nothing in His sight. This walking with God, this conversation in Heaven! Oh how I am ashamed! I sink in silent love. I wonder how the Lord has borne with me for so long. I never had such a view of God and myself. I pray that every moment of my life may show forth His praise.[10]

Is it any wonder that the Societies were doubling during Bramwell's stay in Nottingham?

In Leeds, there was a repetition of the same need, the same intercession, the same blessing. Hull was his next appointment. He writes: "I have had three weeks of agony, but now see the Lord working. I have not preached lately without seeing some fruit of my labor. The Lord is saving souls."[11]

While he was in Hull, a friend offered him the use of a large parlor that overlooked the Humber. To this room he would retire for prayer and quiet, and his host said of his visits: "He was wont to resort frequently to it and spend two, three, four, five, and some-times six hours in prayer and reflection. He often entered the room at nine o'clock in the morning and did not leave it till three in the afternoon. The days on which his longest visits occurred were, I conjecture, his appointed fasts. On these occasions, he refused any kind of refreshment and used to say when he came in, 'Now, take no notice of me.'"

God did a great work through His servant in Sunderland as well, and little wonder, when we read such as the following:

> How is it that the soul being of such value, and God so great, eternity so near, and yet we are so little moved? Perhaps you can

answer me this. Never was I so much struck with the Word of God as at present. The truth, the depth, the promises quite swallow me up. I am lost in wonder and praise. My soul enters into Christ in His blessed Book. His own sayings take faster hold on me than ever. I could read, and weep, and love, and suffer! Yes, what could I not suffer when I thus see Him?

Justification is great; to be cleansed is great; but what is justification, or the being cleansed, when compared to this being taken into Himself? The world, the noise of self, is all gone, and the mind bears the full stamp of God's image. Here you talk and walk and live, doing all in Him and to Him, continuing in prayer and turning all into Christ in every house, in every company.[12]

But this saint of God was no more exempt from very fierce conflicts than we are, as is revealed in the following unburdening of his heart:

I see the greatest necessity of purity in the outward man. To keep the whole requires constant prayer, watching, and looking to Christ. I mean that the soul never be diverted from Him for one moment, but that I view Him in all my acts, take hold of Him as the instrument by which I do all my work, and feel that nothing is done without Him.

To seek men, the world, or self, or praise is so shocking to my view at present, that I wonder we are not all struck dead when the least of this comes upon us. I know immediately when I grieve my Lord; the Spirit speaks within. To do wrong in the clear light is the great offense. My soul is subject to sloth, and I have work, I assure you, to keep all things at full speed.

To another, he writes from Sunderland:

Oh how Satan will tempt you to lie in bed these cold mornings when you should be engaged in prayer and in your study every morning at five o'clock or before. By this practice, what wonders you would do with God, with the Word, with your soul and for your family! Oh arise, my dear brother; you will soon be gone![13]

To young ministers, Mr. Bramwell gave this counsel:

You may be spared to spread the sacred fire when I am in Glory. I am confident much more prayer must be practiced and to greater purpose. In this, I receive every day a greater portion of good from God. I never stood in greater need of praying without ceasing.[14]

His accent on early rising appears again and again. Surely it is no mystery why this man had such power with God and man.

Do you rise about four o'clock every morning? And in order to do this, do you retire to rest as soon as your work and meals are over, or do you sit and chat with the people? Do give yourself to reading and prayer. I say, give, give yourself to these. Are you never in company above an hour at once? When in company, do you turn all into profit—into religion?[15]

His biographer says: "Several of his friends with whom he lodged in the country witnessed, when he left his room in the morning and came to breakfast, that his hair was bedewed with perspiration, as if he had been engaged in the extremity of manual labor. These efforts produced their natural results, and such a wrestling Jacob became a prevailing Israel."

As the end of his earthly ministry approached, the tempo of his prayer life and service increased greatly. From his last appointment, he writes:

I must tell you I am more given to prayer than ever. I feel myself just on the brink of eternity and am sensible I can change nothing when I am gone. This idea being so much with me, I am working with all my might. . . .[16]

Forgive me, when I say to you that my life is now prayer. I feel the need of this continually and can only live in this duty. I hope you will join in this, though absent in the body. A little while, and He will come. You and I will soon have done.[17]

Toward the close of his life, this man of prayer arrived at some very pointed conclusions, which might be applied to the Church of the present day with equal appropriateness.

The reason why the Methodists in general do not live in this salvation is there is too much sleep, too much meat and drink, too little fasting and self-denial, too much conversation with the world, too much preaching and hearing and too little self-examination and prayer.

A number of Methodists now will be in public the whole of the Sabbath, and, if they heard angels all the time, they would be backsliders. It is astonishing how the devil is cheating us, at the same time, filling for a moment our heads and emptying our hearts.

What shall we do? How shall we return? Is it possible to bring the body back by the same way or into the same way? I fear not. I sometimes nearly lose my hope. In all churches, till the present time, Satan has used outward splendor to darken the inward glory. Is it too late to see, to know, to understand the temptations of the devil?[18]

William Bramwell died in Leeds at the close of the Methodist Conference. The last night of his life, he remarked to a group of friends, "It strikes me that one of us will be gone in three or four months."[19] After retiring to his room, he was overheard praying with great earnestness. Again, at two o'clock in the morning, he was pleading with God. Coming downstairs half an hour later, he said to the servant girl who was there, "Praise the Lord! Glory be to God!"[20] He prayed with her before leaving the house and, soon after, not far away, he was found, apparently very ill, by two policemen. Sending one of them for help, he gasped, "Be quick; I shall not be here long."[21]

And so he passed to be with his wonderful Lord with Whom he had communed for so many years. This dear man of God was not yet sixty, but what a legacy he has left all posterity!

Those who have left the deepest impression on this sin-cursed earth have been men and women of prayer.—D. L. Moody.

Those who spend enough time in actual communion with God to become really conscious of their absolute dependence on Him shall change the mere energy of the flesh for the power of God. . . . It is indeed true that he that saveth his time from prayer shall lose it. And he that loseth his time, for communion with God, shall find it again in added blessing and power and fruitfulness.—*John R. Mott.*

Mother Cobb

SAINT IN CALICO

When the fashionable young Mrs. Cobb relinquished her status as a votary of the world and became a lowly servant of Jesus Christ, she startled the inhabitants of Cazenovia, New York. But her decision was only the outward symbol of a profound and deep work of divine grace which marked the beginning of sixty long years of sacrificial and Spirit-inspired living. What chain of circumstances could so permanently have altered the entire course of one who possessed every advantage required of the world for its acceptance?

Eunice Parsons was born into a comfortable home in February, 1793, in Litchfield, Connecticut. Although her parents were not Christians, the eight children were given careful, moral training. The mother was a Universalist; the father, apparently, had little to do with any church.

Mr. Parsons was well established in the business of tailoring and so his daughter became adept at dressmaking. He passed away when Eunice was fourteen, and the mother moved the family to Cazenovia.

The young teenager was attractive, small, with a fair complexion, blue eyes, and wavy golden hair, which she took care to arrange in a way that called attention to her charm. Because of her beauty, she became excessively vain. She loved to hear the swish of her silken dress as she tripped down the aisle of the church, and her clothes were fashioned in the latest style. As she walked along the street in her finery, she was exceedingly conscious of her appearance and careful that every detail of her apparel was as it ought to be. She loved to dance and took pains at all times to maintain a poise and dignity that commanded attention. Her love of fun, together with her personal attractiveness, made her the center of a merry coterie of friends.

However, despite her fondness of the world and its gaieties, she recalled later that, "when but a little child, I felt I ought to love the

Savior and get ready to live with Him in Heaven. I do not remember that I ever neglected to say my little prayer. This text had a great effect upon my feelings: 'Let this mind be in you, which was also in Christ Jesus.'"

When Eunice was twenty-four years of age, she became conscious of the emptiness of the life she was living. Though at that time her knowledge of spiritual truth was meager, she resolved to turn from the pleasures of the world. She frequented the dance no more; she laid aside superfluous adornment and became a member of the Presbyterian Church. A year later, she married Whiteman Cobb, a young man with excellent business prospects. He was not a Christian, but never neglected taking his young wife to church.

During her early married life, the Methodists, "the sect . . . everywhere spoken against," began holding services. Their preaching dealt especially with sin and separation from the world, with a strong emphasis upon holiness of heart as essential to a stable, Christian life and entrance into Heaven as well. When Mrs. Cobb was invited to attend one evening, she accepted, not as some of her friends, to scoff, but to obtain help for her soul. "It was a blessed time," she said. "I witnessed such simplicity, such ardent zeal, such humility, that I said, 'This is the true people of God,' and my heart ran right with them."

In these services, she felt that her spiritual life was so strengthened that, the next year, she told the Presbyterian minister it was her intention to join the Methodists. He argued that whatever spark of heavenly fire she possessed ought to be used to start a flame among the Presbyterians. Her answer was that she herself needed the warmth of a great blaze.

Soon after this, a passage from the book of Hebrews, "Go on unto perfection," rang in her ears. As she waited upon God, He revealed the state of her natural heart, with its workings of pride and love of the world. Although the young woman had adopted a plain style of dress, God showed her that, as far as she personally was concerned, the superfluities of life must be dispensed with. As she prayed, the conviction deepened that the utmost simplicity must henceforth mark her whole deportment. In later life she expressed it thus: "Perfect love dwells only in the bosom of simplicity for, according to the example of Christ and the apostles, true religion is severe in simplicity."

Probably because the love of display had been so prominent in her life, to separate herself completely from all worldly ostentation, Mrs. Cobb resolved to follow the example of Jesus, Who "though he was rich," yet for us "became poor." She decided, to a great extent, to forego the use of her husband's expensive carriage. Instead, she took to walking to her destination, thus identifying herself with the humble poor. She would cut off her beautiful curls and wear a cap. Her dresses were to be made of blue calico.

Though the decision to adopt such a role of poverty was extremely crucifying to her pride, so intense were her longings for cleansing that she resolved to pay the price, whatever the cost. Her yearning heart was satisfied when she went alone to a nearby grove to pray. Her own words describe the conflict which ensued:

> What a struggle I had with the powers of darkness! I was a long time agonizing in prayer. Then I said, "I have done everything that is in my power to do, and I will never rise from this spot till God does the work." Now I was willing to become anything or nothing for Christ's sake.
>
> In that moment, my prayer was answered; my struggle ceased; my unutterable longing was gratified. Instantly a power from above touched me. Jesus took entire possession. I melted as wax before the fire; praise took the place of prayer, and my full soul was dissolved in love. In a moment, I saw that this was sanctification. Oh, what a calm, what a settling down of sweet peace—perfect peace! No ecstasy, only that of astonishment at what I had just realized. It is not in the power of language to describe it. My peace flowed like a river.

Although her path through life was humble and more or less obscure, Mrs. Cobb is outstanding in her exemplification of holiness. Her life breathed out the spirit of prayer. Early in the morning, her family would find her on her knees, with the open Bible before her, seeking divine guidance, as she tells us herself in one of her diary entries:

I arose at four this morning. How clear the mind! How great the happiness in keeping the commandments! "Those that seek me early shall find me." I think this has reference to early in the morning, as well as early in life. It is "the willing and obedient" that eat the "good of the land."

Have some conviction on account of indulgence in bed later than usual this morning. I wonder how I could doze when, if I arise early, I have time for all things. I never saw myself so little, yet I am kept by His almighty power.

Mrs. Cobb persuaded some of her friends to join her every Friday in fasting and prayer for the people of Cazenovia. Once a year, she visited personally every family in the town, praying with them and pointing them to Christ. She stretched out her hand to the needy and, when she herself had no more to give, solicited aid from those who were able to do so.

The course she followed most naturally aroused the opposition of her husband, mother, brothers, and sisters. One who had been an intimate friend passed her by on the other side of the street, not even acknowledging her presence. This hurt her deeply, and for a time the enemy of her soul cruelly taunted her.

One evening, Mrs. Cobb went into her closet to pray, and her disgruntled husband turned the key, locking her in for the night. When he released her the next morning, her reaction to his unkindness was, "Good morning, I have had such a good time praying for you."

Her husband, for a time, made a profession and joined her in worship with the Methodists. For some years, he served as a class leader, and then he grew cold and drifted away. In 1835, he decided to make a home for his family farther west and settled successively near the cities of Laporte, Indiana, and Marengo, Illinois. By these moves, he hoped to separate his wife from those spiritual influences in Cazenovia which he blamed for her very decided religious convictions.

Eunice found life was primitive in both areas to which she moved, but "Mother Cobb," as she came to be known, motivated by her love for souls, went from cabin to cabin, starting prayer services and speaking about the things of God to all who crossed her path. Walking sometimes for miles, this indefatigable soul-winner prayed with the bereaved, visited the sick, and warned the careless. If a fight ensued in the local public house, it quieted the men merely to suggest that Mother Cobb be called to the scene.

Her diary entries reveal how far-reaching were her exertions for the Lord:

> January, 1838. Spent an hour in Chicago, conversing with a number on the importance of being prepared for death. Had a great burden for some young ladies in public houses. Warned them faithfully and prayed for them.
>
> Friday. Was very much blest in visiting the criminals in jail. God gave me an unusual spirit of prayer for my sons and the precious youth of our land.
>
> May 25. I want that holy zeal that when I talk with the unconverted my tears will witness my sincerity. I cannot be idle and grow in grace. I must be exact in redeeming time. I want to breathe the whole spirit of a missionary.

After thirty years of this most faithful sowing, an outpouring of the Holy Spirit attended the ministry of Dr John Redfield throughout this area. And it was apparent to those who knew of the fervent pleadings and tireless efforts of Mother Cobb, that these had prepared the way before it to a degree which only eternity will reveal.

Dr. Redfield's ministry doubtless fulfilled her heart-breathed desire for Spirit-inspired preaching. Mother Cobb's diary discloses her longing:

> I am anxious to witness the pulpit on fire; yes, the pulpit on fire! If anything in the world should be on fire, it is the pulpit. It should glow with intense heat, burning its way to the hearts of the people. The fire should wrap the Book on the sacred desk, leap along the breastwork, and make the floor hot beneath the feet of all occupants.
>
> As the ambassador of Heaven stands there to deliver the Gospel message, his eyes should be eyes of flame, his tongue a fiery tongue, and his whole frame wrapped in fire—fire from the third Heaven—fire from the throne of God. Go, servant of the Lord!

Compel the dwellers by the hedges of sin and in the highways that lead down to Hell.

December 11. Oh, for more laborers in this harvest! And we shall have them when we get this baptism of fire. Oh, the buried talents in all our churches—gifted, educated women, who would be a power for God and their generation while living; and dying, their works would follow them—who are now a mere cipher in the Church for the want of entire living for God. Oh, for more holy women!

We might well ask what was the secret of Mother Cobb's sixty years of such spiritual victory and blessing. It was entire dependence upon God. "I am deeply conscious," she said, "that the root of all sin is having lost God and found self in His place. I do continually see holiness to consist in being sunk into my own nothingness, that God may be exalted in my soul."

In another diary entry, she asks the question:

How am I going to be kept from sin? By the constant application of the blood of Christ, moment by moment. The heart, while it lies in the cleansing fountain, is kept clean. If in doubt, fly to the present, cleansing blood. Claim this prize all anew, moment by moment. I claim all the purchase of Thy blood, because Thou hast promised and art faithful and just to forgive us our sins and to cleanse us from all unrighteousness.

Christ doth not say he that hath come shall never hunger, but he that cometh, indicating a continued and constant coming, a perpetual feeding upon the heavenly bread. Even the hidden manna must ever be eaten, to be ever satisfying; the soul as well as the body must take its daily bread, or it will hunger and pine. So, too, "whosoever drinketh of this water" is he that shall never thirst. Not he that has once tasted and has now forsaken the fountain of living waters is he that never thirsts. The secret of our dissatisfaction is in resting on past experience. Forgetting the things that are behind, let us come every day to Christ and receive anew His life.

Her diary entries reveal deep longings for the repeated baptisms of the Holy Ghost:

I do feel a strong desire for a greater baptism of the Holy Ghost and fire. May it descend upon the Church that we may have the gift of power! What can we do without the living presence, the holy influence? If it be not upon our altars, then we offer vain oblations, and our ceremonies, though instructive, will be lifeless.

December 4. I am before the throne, awaiting the baptism of the Holy Ghost with the power and the fire. Then I shall have strength to labor. Prayers, mighty, importunate, repeated, united prayers; the fathers, the children, the pastor and the people, the rich and the poor, the gifted and the simple, all uniting to cry to God that He may affect us as in the days of the right hand of the Most High and imbue us with the Spirit of Christ and warm and kindle and make us a flame of fire. Such united and repeated supplications will accomplish their end, and the power of God, descending, will make us a band of giants refreshed with new wine.

Mother Cobb had noticed earlier in her life that fasting and prayer obtained results:

For over ten years past, I have been observing the progress of religion among the Methodists, and I find that those who fast and pray most are the most spiritual. Fasting results in quickening the power of faith. In one day, nay in one hour, the whole work may be accomplished. Lord help us!

Oh, what sweet communion I have with the blessed Spirit, not only by day but by night. I do see God in everything. I find it a great blessing to my soul to arise in the night, to pray at twelve. Prayer is just the breath of faith. To pray and not believe is to beat the air. Oh, these crosses taken up in shame and disgrace are borne at last in triumph, even in this life.

Perhaps we do not think enough of prayer—intercessory prayer—direct appeals by names for others, laying their needs—all we desire for them, out before God. We do not believe as we should. How it would help those we would serve, penetrating the heart we cannot open, shielding those we cannot speak to, comforting where our words have no power to soothe, following the steps of our beloved through the toils and perplexities of the day, lifting off their burdens with an unseen hand. At night, no ministry is so like an angel's as this silent, invisible one, known but to God. Through us, descends the blessing and, to Him alone, ascends the thanksgiving. Surely not any employment brings us so near to God as earnest, sincere prayer. There is a depth of wisdom in the words, "If only we spoke more to God for man, than even to man for God."

The little old woman in calico went on, braving all weathers, loving all souls, praying and fasting and enjoying a communion with the Father that brought wealth beyond words. But the separated life had had its moments of pain when even her class leader, failing to understand the motive that controlled this saintly woman, said to her, "Sister Cobb, you are a disgrace to us. Your clothes are not fit to wear in public. If you would dress a little more like other people, you would have a better influence. We bear with you because of your age."

When, during her last illness, several friends called upon her, they asked, "Mother Cobb, has the sting of death been extracted?"

"Yes, Glory!"

"Are you about to change your blue calico for a white robe?"

"Yes. Glory! Glory! Glory!"

"You have been particular in your dress. Don't you think more so than necessary?"

"Oh, no. Glory! Hallelujah! It pays!" Within a few hours, the lips that had moved for blessing on earth were silenced for ever.

QUOTATIONS BY MOTHER COBB

The Scriptures are found so much transcending anything else that we say, as their richness and beauty open before us, with the queen of Sheba on beholding, "The half was not told me." They are more than vases filled with Gilead's balm. They open before us a whole paradise of delight.

Here, in the clefts of the rocks, are droppings of that which is sweeter than honey and the honeycomb. Here the soul finds the tree of life, which is in the midst of the paradise of God. We sit down under His shadow with great delight, and His fruit is sweet to our taste. We pluck eternal peace with God, and escape from the over-spreading deluge of earthly evils, and are led by the hand of Jesus into the ark of eternal refuge.

Felix Neff

THE BRAINERD OF THE HIGH ALPS

"How is it that two hundred years after his death, Protestants of France unite to celebrate the work of an evangelist with neither degree nor diploma and whose ministry in France lasted less than four years? How is it that one of the most isolated valleys in the High Alps became the scene of a mighty work of God, one of the high places of French Protestantism, and the center of an annual gathering of many thousands of people at Freyssinières?" So questioned Mr. G. Williams after a recent trip to those parts.

Felix Neff had much in common with David Brainerd who labored among the American Indians under similar primitive conditions. Both were young. Both came to their field of labor under a cloud of misrepresentation. Both were most self-sacrificing. Both remained unmarried. Both died at an early age from overexertion under conditions of extreme hardship. Both experienced a work of reviving grace. Both were men of prayer.

Felix Neff was born at Geneva, Switzerland, October 8, 1798. He was deprived of his father in early infancy. His mother, although a professed deist, never interfered with her son's early love for the Church. Although her means were limited because of widowhood, she gave him everything possible for his mental development. Tokens of motherly affection were withheld from him save in his sleep, as she wanted to inculcate manly qualities in him.

"I followed the world," said Mrs. Neff, "and my union with a man of brilliant parts and skeptical opinions soon ended in making me, like himself, a deist and an habitual and deliberate neglecter of public worship. Not so was it with my child. At a very early age he delighted to attend the sacred assemblies, and not only did he never fail doing so, but was remarkable for the seriousness of his deportment. Happily, he never asked me why I did not go."[1]

Felix was self-taught in botany, history, and geography. From his pastor, he gained some knowledge in Latin. He was gifted with a most retentive memory, truthful to a fault, but was strong-willed and haughty. Because the local village schoolmaster lacked a proper education, the mother became tutor to her son.

Before the lad was thirteen, they moved to Cartigny. Felix had, by this time, exhausted the library of which their home could boast, as well as any other books his mother could acquire for him. An effort to locate him in a good school failed in its endeavor. As employment was most difficult to procure, the teenage lad occupied his leisure hours studying insect life and trees and wrote a treatise on the care of the latter. He also continued his mathematical and Latin studies. He had read Plutarch and Rousseau from the age of eight until he was sixteen, but their infidel arguments did not seem to affect him.

But God was preparing His instrument. His mother writes, "I had always left him to follow his own inclinations. Alas, I saw not the Hand which controlled us both, leading me to send him to the good Pastor Montinie, who soon appreciated his character and anxiously wished to be of service to him. His endeavors were, however, fruitless, and we, being nearly destitute of pecuniary resources, he advised my son to enter the army." [2]

Here, by his seriousness and application to work, Felix was rapidly advanced to the rank of sergeant, much to the chagrin of those who had been training much longer. His Captain once said to him, "You leave nothing for the soldiers to do—you have no idea of commanding." "It is the best and surest way of commanding," replied the youth. [3]

From an early age, he had fixed ideas of the evils of the world. "Do you think there is no amusement at a theater?" queried a friend. "On the contrary, I think there is too much," was the reply. [4]

A growing conviction that the spring of all his actions was selfish, caused him in deep distress to pray, "Oh, my God, whatsoever Thou art, make me to know Thy truth; vouchsafe to manifest Thyself to me." [5]

He began a diligent study of the Bible, as it seemed to him that no other book could unlock the mysteries regarding the unregenerate state of the human heart. To him as yet, however, God was a stern Judge, not a merciful Father.

Then, through a book, *Honey Flowing from the Rock*, loaned to him by his pastor, Felix at last received spiritual understanding. It was written by an Englishman, Thomas Willcock. This passage brought balm to the young man:

> If you knew Jesus Christ, you would not for all the world wish to do a single good work without Him (II Cor. 3:5). If you already know Him, you know that He is the Rock of salvation, infinitely above any righteousness of our own (Psa. 61:2). This Rock will follow you everywhere (I Cor. 10:4). From this Rock flows the honey of grace, which alone can satisfy you. Would you go to Jesus? Renounce all idea of your own goodness, taking with you nothing but your misery and sin.
>
> Would you know all the horrors of sin? Do not be content to examine its extent in yourself. Go to Jesus on the cross; behold in His sufferings the malignity of sin and tremble. Let the Spirit of God guide you in the study of the Bible. It is a mine wherein the most precious treasure is hid, even the knowledge of Christ.[6]

Written on the margin of the book were the words, "Felix Neff has found peace here on these two pages." And of the experience he wrote:

> When after a thousand useless vows and a thousand ineffective efforts, I learned at last that in me dwells no good thing, I was happy indeed to run across a book which depicted with exact truth the miserable state of my heart and showed me at the same time the only efficacious remedy. I received with joy the good news, that we should go to Christ with all our stains, all our unbelief, and all our impenitence.[7]

Although the energetic convert was far from satisfied with the spiritual condition of the national Church of Switzerland, he was not a separatist and sought by holding *réunions*—Bible studies and prayer meetings—within the established Church, to deepen its spiritual life.

During the day, Felix would work in the vineyards and, at evening, he would speak to peasants gathered to hear him. Speaking of his labors in Switzerland he writes:

> I spoke of evangelical simplicity in opposition to barren theology.[8] . . . The whole of this Canton seems preparing for a great revival, at least, if one may judge by the agitation of Satan.[9]
>
> I have already held thirteen prayer meetings in seven different villages, and they have been attended by half the population of the place. In the intervals, I visit all the pious Christians in their own houses and those who are as yet but inquiring.[10]

He saw clearly that the world would tolerate its followers professing merely a belief in the Bible, but would severely punish those who sought to govern their lives by its precepts. Therefore he spoke everywhere of the necessity of separation from the world.

These unpopular tenets which the young exhorter held and taught first surprised and then enraged the ministers who would not allow any religious teaching not under their direct supervision. In a conversation with a local deacon he defended his position:

> I remarked that I could not see how prayer meetings, carried on without any regular system, without a liturgy, or without the celebration of sacraments, could be in any way detrimental to the interests or tranquillity of the established minister, adding that either the established minister receives his authority from men or from God. If he receives it from men, we have no occasion to respect it as divine. If he receives it from God, let him prove that he does so, by respecting all that God does to promote the advancement of His heavenly kingdom, and not arrogate himself the right of prescribing to God the means He is to use for the accomplishment of this purpose.[11]

Ill health forced Felix Neff to leave the Jura without delay. In Neuchatel, opposition to his *réunions* caused him to record in his diary, on Jan. 10, 1821, "I have just received permission to remain till

5th of April; many are very angry, but hitherto government tolerates me, and the Lord appears to have opened many hearts."[12]

A providence brought him to the notice of M. Blanc, pastor of Mens, in France. An interview was arranged, and Neff observed, "I informed him that I never pursued any regular course of study and that I should certainly never be ordained at Geneva. He did not seem to think the worse of me for this and invited me to visit him at Mens. . . . He even would like me to pass some months there, in the absence of his colleague."[13]

At twenty-four years of age, Neff left his native Switzerland for France, where the few Protestants were poorly provided with clergy. He labored for six months as an assistant to a pastor in Grenoble, holding *réunions* as he had done in the Jura, Switzerland. Of these Neff writes:

> I am more and more convinced that these *réunions* are a very efficacious means of promoting practical piety. They encourage mutual confidence, humility, simplicity, and brotherly love. It is an error of pride and presumption to suppose that we have nothing to do with the spiritual affairs of our brethren. On the contrary, we are all members of the same body, and therefore members of one another, and if one of the members suffer, all the other members suffer with it. . . .
>
> I know by experience that the dead and lifeless state of which we all complain is occasioned by our own fault. We either do not pray, or we are not persevering and assiduous in prayer. . . . Our heart being naturally at a distance from God, it is not a single step that will bring us near to Him, neither will a few minutes of cold prayer suffice to support our souls.[14]

In 1822, the young evangelist removed to Mens and assisted M. Blanc in instructing the catechumens who numbered seventy. Once a week the young assistant visited them, only one-fifth of whom resided at Mens, the remainder being scattered in twenty different villages in almost impassable country. He was very disappointed to discover "not one single ripe ear of corn" in so large a harvest field and bemoaned the worldly spirit which predominated. He writes:

There is little spiritual life in this place, and even B. himself, I cannot help thinking, seems too well satisfied that he is a Protestant and to be content with that. . . . I can perceive he is afraid I should establish prayer meetings, for he often talks to me of the danger of innovations, and of going too far. . . . I am, however, thankful that he approves of the true and wholesome doctrines of the Gospel, and I trust that the Lord will yet further open his eyes. . . . Invited into society, I hear nothing but worldly conversation, for B. never introduces religious subjects, except for the purpose of controversy.[15]

Neff's courageous and faithful teaching began to reap results. Some striking cases of deep conviction, culminating in salvation, encouraged the evangelist. Something akin to a revival took place affecting a large area.

There were disheartening setbacks. A long letter from a minister in Geneva to M. Blanc, delineating Neff's faults and shortcomings, warned the pastor to take care of wolves in sheep's clothing. Then the absent minister, for whom Neff had acted as substitute, returned and sought reinstatement. Some reluctance among the people to do this resulted in party spirit, the minister openly misrepresenting Felix Neff and deriding his rigid sentiments. This influenced some who had given bright promise. About one hundred families, fearing that their faithful catechist would leave them, offered to raise a stipend for him. These considered him a saint, but their praise wounded Neff quite as much as had the misrepresentations.

M. Blanc was very tolerant of his young assistant to whom he would at times unburden his heart. Even the reproofs Neff administered from time to time were received in a gracious manner, for M. Blanc had come to know the sterling worth of the young man, who was undeterred by inclement weather and who never thought of himself. Summing up Neff's ministry in Mens, he wrote:

Gifted with great natural abilities, especially with an unusual degree of eloquence and, having his heart warmed with love of his Savior, he preached several times in the course of a day, but never repeated the same discourse.[16]

During his residence among us of nearly two years, he was instrumental in effecting the greatest good. Zeal for religion increased; many people were brought seriously to think of their immortal souls; the Bible was more deeply searched and carefully read; the catechumens were better informed in their Christian duties and showed their improvement by their conduct; family worship was established in many houses; the love of luxury and vanity greatly diminished . . . schools were established . . . a visible improvement had taken place in the manners and industrious habits of our Protestants. . . .[17]

In order to be more acceptable to the Church in France, Neff sought ordination. But he could not receive it there, because of his irregular studies. So he applied to a body of pastors of the Independent Congregations in England who granted his request.

Upon his return from England, Neff was to learn that suspicions regarding his being ordained abroad had spread. He was misrepresented as a hidden enemy with foreign religious connections who was disseminating new doctrines. The local magistrate had had the *réunions* misrepresented to him and requested that these be discontinued. So Neff looked elsewhere for a field of labor. He preached his farewell sermon on, "We must through much tribulation enter into the kingdom." Turning his thoughts to the High Alps, Neff wrote: "Among the Alps I should be the sole pastor. In the south, I should be surrounded by pastors, many of them on good terms with the world and should be constantly annoyed."[18]

After much difficulty as to naturalization and a permit to labor, the ardent evangelist finally, at the age of twenty-six, began the work for which he is most remembered. For a few years, in order to feed the scattered flock of God, he constantly traveled back and forth over dangerous mountain passes in the highest and coldest parish in all France.

One of his journeys described in his journal will give us some conception of the difficulties of travel. The day was stormy, and the villagers entreated the young minister not to cross the *col* [mountain pass] in such weather. But Neff, feeling he must preach at Dormilleuse at the appointed time, procured a guide and, armed with a large stick, approached the mountain. He writes:

> It requires the pen of a poet to describe the awful and magnificent scenery. We were knee deep in snow. A storm of hail, driven by a sharp wind, accompanied the repeated claps of thunder, and the rolling of the avalanches falling from the highest rocks. The lightning flashed above and below us, and the drifts of snow threatened to overwhelm us.
>
> Happily, all this storm was at our backs, and there was no precipice near us. We, therefore, were in no real danger. At last we reached the *col*, where we found snow three feet deep and the wind insupportable. We arrived at the descent, and I then dismissed my guide and continued to descend, still up to my knees in snow. A fog arose, and I could just see the points of the rocks gilded with the rays of the sun. I then sang a few verses of the "Te Deum" and, quickening my pace, I discovered the tracks of some sheep driven into the valley by the snow. I arrived by daylight at Dormilleuse, where they were not a little surprised to see me.

In a letter to a friend, he describes the historical and moral setting of the people among whom he worked:

> This village (Dormilleuse), the highest in the valley of Freyssinières, is celebrated for the stout resistance which its inhabitants, for more than sixty years, have made against the encroachments of the Church of Rome. They are the lineal, unadulterated descendants of the Vaudois and never bowed their knees to Baal.
>
> . . . The remains of forts and walls, which they had built to prevent the enemy from surprising them, are still to be seen. And the almost inaccessible nature of their country was also a great means of their preservation. The population of this village is entirely Protestant, as well as that of the other villages of the valley. The aspect of this country, at once dreadful and sublime, which afforded a shelter to truth while the rest of the world lay in darkness; the recollection of those ancient and faithful martyrs, whose blood even now stains the rocks; the deep caverns whither they retired to read the Scriptures and to worship the Father of light in

spirit and in truth—all tend to elevate the soul and excite feelings and emotions impossible to describe.

But these thoughts soon give place to grief, when the mind's eye rests on the present condition of the descendants of those ancient witnesses of the crucified Jesus. They are degenerated in every sense of the word. And their state reminds the Christian that sin and death are all that the sons of Adam can really bequeath to their descendants. And, alas, that inheritance is inalienable.

A great respect for the Scripture is, nevertheless, kept up amongst them, and we must hope that they are still "beloved for their fathers' sakes," and that the Lord will again cause His face to shine upon that place, which He chose for His sanctuary. . . .

The work of an evangelist in High Alps greatly resembles that of a missionary among the savages, the almost equal degree of uncivilization that prevails among them both, being a great obstacle to missionary labors. Among the valleys, under my charge, that of Freyssinières is the most backward. Architecture, agriculture, education of every sort is in its very earliest infancy.

Many houses are without chimneys, and many without windows. All the family, during the seven winter months, stow themselves into the stable, which is only cleaned once a year. Their dress and food are equally coarse and unwholesome. Their bread, which is made once a year, consists of the coarsest rye. . . . If any of them are ill, they have no doctor, and no one to administer either medicine or sick food. . . . The invalid may think himself happy if he can obtain a draught of water.

The women are harshly treated, as among people still in a barbarous state. They seldom sit down, but generally kneel or crouch down. They never sit at table or eat with the men, who give them a piece of bread over their shoulder without looking around—a miserable pittance, which they receive with a low reverence, kissing the hand of the giver.

The inhabitants of these melancholy villages were so wild when I first came among them that, at the sight of a stranger, even a peasant, they would run away into their huts. The young people, especially the girls, were unapproachable.

With all this, this people participated in the general corruption, as far as poverty would permit. Gambling, dancing, swearing, quarreling are to be met with here as elsewhere. . . .[19]

There is scarcely a house that is proof against the snow drifts and pieces of falling rock. From the period of my arrival, I conceived a peculiar affection for this valley and felt an ardent desire to become, as it were, an Oberlin to the poor people. Unfortunately, I was not able to spend more than a week with them in the course of a month.

Felix Neff, in his short period of service, helped to build schools and churches for worship. He also taught improved methods of potato culture and introduced irrigation, assisting in its implementation. He founded schools and secured teachers, but it was for the spiritual reviving of this people that he travailed.

A genuine movement of the Spirit was noticed when he visited Freyssinières. It seemed as though the whole valley had assembled, and a solemnity and awe rested upon the entire congregation. Passing on to other villages, he witnessed still further proofs of a moving of the Spirit:

All the people seemed to give themselves up to reading, meditation, and prayer; the young people especially seemed animated by a holy spirit; a heavenly flame appeared to have communicated itself from one to another. I had scarcely thirty hours' rest during the week. . . .

Struck with astonishment at the apparent suddenness of this awakening, I could scarcely believe my senses. Even the rocks, the cascades, and the ice seemed inspired with life and offered up to my eye a less dismal and gloomy prospect than formerly. This wild country has become dear and delightful to me, now that it has become the habitation of Christian brethren.[20]

The exertions of this lowly ambassador of Christ had taken a heavy toll. Writing in his journal, he remarks:

It was not till the Spring of 1828 that I began first to perceive my stomach sensibly weakened by the coarse food and irregularity of my meals, and perhaps in some degree, too, by the uncleanliness of the cookery utensils used in this country. . . .

My constant Alpine journeys were both painful and dangerous, on account of the severity of the winter. . . .Constant internal pains and indigestion obliged me to observe an abstinence but ill-suited to the fatigue and cold to which I was exposed. A sprained knee, brought on by walking across the fragments of an immense avalanche, suddenly arrested my course about the end of March. . . . I soon perceived that it was absolutely necessary to seek medical assistance—assistance which, with all their good will, these poor mountaineers could not procure me.[21]

In 1827, at only twenty-nine years of age, the sick man left his beloved people for Geneva. After the first few months of rest, he rallied so much that people did not believe him to be ill. But a relapse set in toward Spring. It altered him so much that old friends scarcely knew him, and strangers took his mother for his wife, although she was sixty-seven.

As the untiring worker now reviewed his years of labor, he could see how he had overstrained his body by incessant labors:

> This interruption of my activity is a trial I well deserve. I often feared, in the midst of my greatest vigor, that I placed too much confidence in my strength and pleased myself too much in a power of action which nothing seemed capable of interrupting or wearying, and that I thus ran the risk of one day being deprived of it, for the sake of my spiritual good.[22]

How often in those days of enforced rest he longed to be back in the High Alps. He wrote:

> In spirit I often revisit your valleys and long to be able to endure cold and fatigue, to sleep in a stable on a bed of straw, in order to proclaim the Word of God. . . .
>
> My words have often wearied you, and my plainness of speech has often offended you, and many of you saw me depart with joy. But were I still amongst you, I should not change my language. Truth is unchangeable. I should still entreat you, in the name of Jesus, to be reconciled to God.[23]

No murmur was heard to pass his lips during those long, long months of illness. During the last weeks of his life, he endured agony and could not bear reading or receiving visitors. He was heard to whisper, "Victory, victory, victory in Jesus Christ," as the end approached. Felix Neff then passed from the scene of his short labors to receive the Master's "Well done."

What was the secret of this young man's endurance under such hardship, toil, and misunderstanding? Early in his Christian life, he had understood that going "without the camp" is the lot of every dedicated Christian. He had armed his mind with the thought that we must fill up the sufferings of Christ.

Writing in all frankness to his close friend, M. Blanc, he reveals his inner attitude toward this subject:

> I have often told you why you find it so difficult to endure the hatred, contempt, and perfidy of the world. It is because you cannot bring yourself to believe that thus it must be, and that this continual struggle is inseparable from the Gospel. It is because, on entering the ministry, you did not take this into consideration, but rather reckoned on the esteem of men, on worldly ease and comfort. My case is different.
>
> When my eyes first opened to the bright light of the Gospel, it was a critical moment, and I saw nothing but the rage and fury of the wolf against the sheep of the Good Shepherd and I now think nothing of the little contradiction I meet with. Nevertheless, I wish not to boast, for if, by the grace of God, I have some strength, I have but little in comparison with other laborers a thousand times more faithful than I am. And besides, I have so many causes for humiliation that I must be worse than a fool to esteem myself on any account.[24]
>
> All I can do is to point to the Giver of every good and perfect gift—to Him, Who when He came to open the kingdom of Heaven to us was far from having His earthly path strewed with roses and met with but little honor and respect. . . .
>
> Do not, I entreat you, talk of "an end of all this," of "Satan being conquered" etc. Either lay down your arms and submit at once to the enemy, or make up your mind to a life of warfare. If outward peace were to be granted you, I should fear that spiritual life would soon expire. . . . Perfect peace in this world is death to the new man. . . . For our flesh—no peace, no repose, no honor, no esteem.[25]

QUOTATIONS BY FELIX NEFF

To those who have found rest to their souls in Jesus Christ, but those whose spiritual life has gradually become feeble and languishing, I say without hesitation that this evil arises from their neglect of prayer and meditation. They are content to know these things without practicing them. They speak of the grace of God, but they seek it not. They know Jesus Christ, but they do not cultivate a close communion with Him. They are not sufficiently Christians in private. They do not seek Christ in their closets. It is in vain to expect to find God in the temple, if He does not accompany us there.

The source of life is not in ourselves. It is in God and in proportion as we neglect to apply to this source, by prayer, reading, and meditation, we shall become dry and unfruitful, just as a meadow in a sandy soil, and exposed to the sun would languish and fade for want of water.[26]

"Abide in me." It is not given to any creature to have life in itself. It is only in proportion as Christ dwells in us, and we in Him, that we have any real life in us.[27]

Robert Cleaver Chapman

THE RICH, POOR MAN

"Leave Robert Chapman alone; we talk about heavenly places; but he lives in them." This was the response given when some critic was attempting to determine where Mr. Chapman stood as regards the controversy which was then raging in the Christian Brethren Movement. And true it is that R. C. Chapman shines out above all parties and differences, as a man of God, loving but uncompromising, gentle but searching, humble but one who spoke with authority, gifted but utterly childlike, self-effacing but never-to-be-forgotten.

What was his secret? In the few available accounts concerning his early Christian life, apart from his conversion, there is an utter dearth of personal testimony. The purposeful destruction of his papers leave on display the "fruit of the Spirit" dangling before us most appetizingly, but tending to keep the branch out of sight. The key to the secret of his beautiful Christian life is evident, however, for his passion was, whatever the cost, to be a Bible Christian. And that cost was the Cross of Christ.

Robert Cleaver Chapman was the son of Thomas Chapman of Whitby on the Yorkshire coast. His father was a wealthy merchant whose family boasted an ancient coat of arms. At the time of Robert's birth in 1803, the family was resident in Elsinore, Denmark. The lad grew up surrounded by luxury, and no one could have imagined that his mature years would be spent in a small house in a poor, working-class district, and that he would be utterly dependent upon God for the supply of every temporal need.

Upon the return of the family to England, Robert's education was continued at a respectable boarding school in Yorkshire. At fifteen, he left for London where, as an apprentice clerk, he studied law. The surroundings and the daily tasks were far from congenial to an out-of-doors lad from the north. But young Chapman determined to make a success of the legal profession and, by long hours and diligent application (qualities later applied to his study of God's Word), he became an attorney at the early age of twenty.

Being a Chapman of Whitby, he was admitted into fashionable circles and often invited to select parties. His rapidly developing poise and confidence bid fair to make him a popular and much sought-after young man in society.

He was not, however, immune to thoughts of religion. He had read the Bible carefully and, convinced that it was the Word of God, endeavored to keep the law and to find salvation by good works.

In a letter written to Mr. Gladstone when Chapman was ninety-one years of age, he said, "The undersigned, in his youth, sought diligently and with strong purpose, to establish his own righteousness, in hope thereby to obtain eternal life. In the eyes of all who knew him, he had become a blameless young man, and devout."

Gradually he began to see the hopelessness of obtaining God's approval in this way. "I hugged my chains," he said. "I would not—could not—hear the voice of Jesus. My cup was bitter with my guilt and the fruit of my doings. Sick was I of the world, hating it in vexation of spirit, while yet I was unable and unwilling to cast it out."

Churchman though Robert was, he accepted the invitation of a deacon of John Street Chapel to hear the eloquent and godly pastor, James Harrington Evans, a former clergyman of the Church of England. Reluctantly the young man assented, wondering what type of service was conducted by the nonconformists. The sermon shattered his confidence in his own righteousness:

> What shall we think of him who is building his hopes of pardon, acceptance, and salvation upon his own wretched and miserable doings? What shall we think of him who, instead of building on the safe and sure foundation of a crucified Savior, is building on tears, on prayers, on almsdeeds, on religious, or rather, irreligious services, who builds his expectations of Heaven upon the ruins of God's holy law, and thinks that in order to save him, God must "undeify" Himself?
>
> All this is sand—treacherous, yielding sand, for it is as possible for God to cease to be, as to cease to be just. "A just God and a

Savior, there is none beside me." An unjust God is no God, and he who tramples on His own law is no better.

As the young lawyer listened to Pastor Evans' message he felt his edifice of good works crumbling around him, and he was enabled by divine grace to trust only in the merits of his Savior. What peace and joy flooded his heart! In his own words, "In the good and set time Thou spakest to me, saying, 'This is the rest wherewith ye may cause the weary to rest; and this is the refreshing.' And how sweet Thy words, 'Son, be of good cheer; thy sins be forgiven thee!' How precious the sight of the Lamb of God, and how glorious the robe of righteousness, hiding from the holy eyes of my Judge all my sin and pollution!"

Few could have imagined the future servant of God in the young man who ascended the pulpit steps one Sunday morning to tell, earnestly and simply, what had taken place in his life. His sky-blue, swallow-tailed coat, with large gilt buttons, marking him as a member of the fashionable set, was startling to the staid congregation. But a solemn hush settled over them, as he told of his newfound peace.

Someone has said that the first twenty-four hours of a convert's history may well determine the future quality of his Christianity. And Chapman gave immediate promise of becoming a wholehearted, other-world follower of the Lord Jesus Christ. In his *Meditations* he writes:

> The offense of the Cross hath not ceased. No sooner did I know Thee and confess Thee, than I became a stranger to the sons of Hagar, who gender only to bondage, whose child I was by nature. Thy love drew me aside from the path of the worldly, whether wicked or devout. I became an offense to those I forsook, even those of my own flesh and blood. And wherefore were they angry? Because, in taking up my Cross, I became a witness against them by my boasting only in Thee, and counting all who are of the works of the law to be under the curse.

In all this opposition, Mr. Chapman was helped by the warm, spiritual atmosphere of the chapel and the keen interest and care of the pastor whom he grew to love and even unconsciously tried to imitate in preaching, but with little success. He especially valued and drew strength from the weekly breaking of bread.

Pastor Evans had early seen the dangers of spiritual pride in his own life and now, through grace, consistently and honestly regarded himself "less than the least of all saints." Through his influence, a deep hunger to be as nothing that he might "win Christ," took hold of young Chapman. As a result, he soon was following his lowly Master in ministering to the poor and grossly sinful. Instead of attending gay parties as previously, he spent evenings which were not devoted to the study of the Bible, in reaching the destitute in the districts around Gray's Inn Lane. This only widened the gulf between him and his former friends, as well as most of his relatives.

For three years, his worldly prospects improved, and he began to practice as a solicitor on his own account. His gracious manner and keen intelligence assured him of much success. However, at twenty-nine years of age, he knew God was calling him to sell all his possessions, give away his private fortune, and devote his entire time to His service.

He accepted an invitation to become the pastor of a Strict Baptist Chapel in Barnstable, Devon. Upon his arrival, he secured temporary lodgings in a humble house on a side street. Later he rented one in New Buildings, not far from the chapel, but just over the wall from a tannery, which emitted the most disagreeable odors.

A relative of Chapman's, in fact the only one who deigned to visit him in this place, hired a cab to take him there. When dropped off at Number 6, he assured the cabman there must be a mistake, for this could not possibly be the home of Robert Chapman!

But, when converted, Chapman had realized that pride was his besetting sin. So, in his hatred of that evil principle, in the very town where he had once driven with relatives in a carriage with coachmen and footmen, he chose to live in a working man's cottage on a side street. "My pride never got over it," he once admitted.

He most solemnly remarked at one time that it was a pity there were so few D.D.'s.

"Surely not!" returned a somewhat shocked brother.

"Yes," was the reply. "We want more people in Psalm 119: 25, 'Down in the dust.' Then we would also have more quickened, 'according to thy word.'"

The young bachelor, persuaded that God wanted his small home to be a "guest house" for Christian people, threw the doors wide open to any who came. And when, for a period of time, none appeared, he "prayed" them in. The question of room never worried him in the least, and his observation was, "The Lord takes care of that." And He surely did, for none ever were turned away.

Chapman took upon himself to polish the boots and shoes of his guests. When some protested, he insisted that Jesus taught us to wash the saints' feet, and that in modern civilization the nearest approach to obedience to that command was to black their boots.

Such became the reputation of the presence and outflowing of love in his humble cottage that a letter from abroad addressed to R. C. Chapman, University of Love, England, actually was delivered to his door.

An American guest, who took a short "course" at this institution of heavenly learning, wrote of Chapman's rising at three-thirty in the morning, of his spending the entire forenoon in prayer and Bible study, interspersed necessarily with the preparation of breakfast, lighting of fires, and other household tasks. His host's combination of authority and humility was most amazing. It seemed that Mr. Chapman expounded the Scriptures almost as an oracle. And yet, when he accompanied his guest to the station, he hung on his every word, as though he could not afford to miss anything that would give further spiritual enlightenment.

Chapman's communion and fellowship with God were most intimate. "When I bow to God, God stoops to me," he declared. "As the father and child do all they can to please each other, so I do all I can to please God, and God does all He can to please me."

He was told of a "perfectionist" who said he had reverted to the state of Adam, born without sin and with only the possibility, in an unguarded moment, of wrongdoing.

"Adam's state!" he exclaimed with vehemence. "Back to Adam's state! I would not change places with Adam before the Fall for a hundred thousand worlds."

Chapman cultivated the grace of brotherly love. His one friendly relative, while visiting him, looked into his larder and asked if he might obtain some groceries for him. Chapman consented on condition that he purchase them from a certain shopkeeper whom he named. This merchant, gratified by the largeness of the order, was discomfited and totally incredulous when told it was to be delivered to Chapman whom he detested. After delivering the groceries, this man, who had formerly made Chapman the target of his abuse, was discovered prostrate on his face before the man of God in tears, begging forgiveness.

When told of the fault of another, Chapman was wont to say, "Let us go to our brother and tell him of this." One day, a member of the chapel called on him, expressing distress at the conduct of a certain sister. He listened and, as she concluded her grievances, retired from the room for a few minutes. Returning with his overcoat and Bible, he remarked, "I'm going now."

"But, Mr. Chapman, I came for your advice."

"I will give it," was his reply, "when you come with me to call on the sister. You see, I never judge by appearance but must always hear both sides."

The visitor accompanied him most reluctantly but, after the three had conversed awhile, she humbly confessed her lack of love.

When anyone in his presence criticized the public address of a speaker, his reaction was, "Let us tell him so," at the same time rising from his chair. This attitude, in a very effective way, dampened further criticism and made his parishioners understand his hatred of talebearing.

On one occasion, when he was calling from house to house with one of his church members, he met a woman who felt it her duty to give him a most severe tongue-lashing. He listened for a while, with no comment. Then he called to his colleague across the street, "Dear brother, listen to this sister, she is telling me all that is in her heart." Needless to say, her stream of vituperation dried up at once.

God granted a long and useful life to His servant. He preached his last sermon just before his ninety-eighth birthday. At the ripe old age of ninety-nine years, Robert Chapman passed away with the words upon his lips, "The peace of God, which passeth all understanding."

Doubtless the treasury of Christian literature is the poorer because Robert Chapman, in a spirit of self-abnegation, destroyed most of his papers. However, from the limited supply available, the few quotes we do include reveal the character of the man.

Our need of prayer is as frequent as the moments of the day, and as we grow in spirituality of mind, our continual need will be felt by us more and more.

It is a great help to us when we see that our prayers and our labors are to be as the grain of wheat falling into the ground. If we look for death and burial first, we shall be able to go on in patience, and in due time shall assuredly reap an abundant harvest. One of the best answers to prayer is to be able to continue in prayer. To be strong in faith, two things are needful—a very low esteem of ourselves and a very high esteem of Christ.

What is most precious in the sight of God is often least noticed by men.

To rise above the first Adam, we must live in the last Adam. We shall then be able in spirit to use the language of the 8th Psalm, and have all things under our feet.

The ruin of a kingdom is a little thing in God's sight in comparison with division among a handful of sinners redeemed by the blood of Christ.

A good workman gains skill by his mistakes.

Christ twice passed the angels by. He sank far below them in His humiliation; He rose far above them in His exaltation.

THE CONTRITE HEART

The contrite heart is incense sweet,
    Our gracious God, to Thee;
It worships at thy mercy-seat
    In perfect liberty.

The contrite heart is large and deep,
    Thy mysteries it knows;
On Calvary abides to weep,
    And shares in Thy repose.

Fit dwelling of the heav'nly Dove
    Trembling with holy fear;
For Christ the Bridegroom, sick of love,
    It waits till He appear.

Image express of Thy dear Son,
    The now exalted Lamb;
It meekly says, "Thy will be done,"
    And sanctifies Thy name.

It yields a note in ev'ry sigh,
    Of melody divine,
To which attent, O God, Most High,
    Thou dost Thine ear incline.

That gift which Thou wilt not despise
    Do Thou to us impart;
And then accept our sacrifice—
    A broken, contrite heart.
            —*R. C. Chapman.*[1]

To have nothing and to be nothing, this is riches, quietness, rest. —*R. C. Chapman.*

Holy Ann

THE IRISH SAINT

"Poor Ann, she can never learn anything!" exclaimed the school teacher in a despairing way. The small girl had been in the class just one week, but found the ABC's so difficult to master that the conclusion was reached that effort on such a dull child was utterly wasted. So she was summarily dismissed, to return to her humble Irish cottage, with its thatched roof, in Ballamacally, County Armagh, Ireland. And yet, in mature years, Ann came to be known for her wide knowledge of the Bible and a record of answers to her simple prayers of faith that silenced the most faithless and unbelieving cavilers.

Religion was unheeded in the home into which she was born in the year 1810. The six children who came to James Preston and his wife were forced to seek employment as soon as they were able and, since Ann could not imbibe even the simplest principles of education, she was hired out for infant caring or cattle herding, for the most part, in families of the God-forgetting. Finally, she was taken into a Christian home, where the mistress was concerned about the spiritual welfare of all who came under her roof. At her invitation, the servant girl attended a Methodist class meeting, where some of the members were weeping because of their sins, while others were praising God for saving grace.

To Ann's mind, so completely ignorant of anything spiritual, this gathering was repellent. However, she consented to go to a Methodist service in a private home the following Sunday. The text of the minister was that command of our Savior, "Thou, when thou prayest, enter into thy closet, and when thou hast shut thy door, pray to thy Father which is in secret; and thy Father which seeth in secret shall reward thee openly." That evening, hardly knowing why, she resorted to a small attic room and, kneeling by the only chair there, broke out into loud crying. Her mistress, suspecting the trouble, ascended the stairs with the question, "What is the matter, Ann?"

"I don't know," was the response. However, it was quickly followed by the confession, "Yes, I do. I see the sins I did from the time I was five years old, all written on the chair in front of me, every one. Worse than all, I see Hell open ready to swallow me."

In the great agitation of her soul, now awakened to its true state before God, she retired to her own room where, until midnight, she continued to cry out to Him for mercy. Then, as the question, "No mercy, Lord, for me?" passed her lips, divine assurance was given her that through the blood of Jesus, her sins were washed away.

She picked up a New Testament lying on the table and, placing her finger on a verse, prayed, "Father, You Who have taken away from me this awful burden, couldn't You help me read one of these little things?" And a miracle was wrought! Ann was able to read at least part of the verse, "Whosoever drinketh of this water shall thirst again: but whosoever drinketh of the water that I shall give him shall never thirst."

And eventually she, who had been condemned by her childhood teacher to lifelong ignorance, was given the ability to read the Word of God. However, for reasons known only to our Heavenly Father, He never opened the door of her mind to secular reading matter. One family for whom Ann worked, refused to believe that such an unusual situation could exist. To test her veracity, they placed a newspaper in front of her, asking her to read a certain paragraph. She made no progress, until the word "lord" arrested her attention. Then she exclaimed, "It seems to me this word is 'lord,' but it can't be my Lord, for my heart does not burn while I read it." Lord Roberts, who figured prominently in the South African War, was the gentleman about whom the article was written.

In the course of time, Ann was employed in the home of a Dr. Reid whose wife was a Christian. When the family decided to move to Canada, she was invited to accompany them. Much to the grief of her parents, she consented. After a journey of two months, the Reids, together with Ann, settled in Thornhill, Ontario, not far from the city of Toronto.

With all the changes she had undergone, the religious life of the Irish servant girl seemed almost to have come to a standstill, although she still professed to be a Christian. Mrs. Phoebe Palmer, outstanding for her advocacy of the doctrine of holiness, was, for a time, leader of the class meeting in the Methodist Church at Thornhill. Ann reluctantly yielded to Mrs. Reid's persuasions to accompany her to the service.

She had been with the Reid family for about ten years, when the wife and mother suddenly passed away. The family of young children was left to Ann's care, and she was faithful to her trust until they reached maturity and left the home nest.

Neither Dr. Reid nor Ann had attained to any great degree of stability in the Christian life. She, to her sorrow, frequently gave way to violent outbursts of temper when the children tried her patience. Dr. Reid's inconsistency with the profession of religion he maintained annoyed Ann greatly at times. On occasion, in family prayers, she placed her fingers in her ears to avoid hearing his voice. Sinning and repenting seemed to be the best she could hope for, until light from God showed her a life completely victorious over sin.

A young Christian visiting Dr. Reid was asked to conduct the regular family evening worship. As he read the 34th Psalm, the sixteenth verse spoke very strongly to Ann: "The face of the Lord is against them that do evil, to cut off the remembrance of them from the earth." The young man, at her request, turned down the corner of the page upon which the verse was found. Ann went at once to her room, opened the Bible, and began to pray that God would show her what it meant. The great enemy of souls whispered, "But you can't read it."

In simple faith she replied, "The Lord will give it to me." Again a miracle took place. Ann could read the verse! Continuing in prayer, she asked, "What is evil?" Then followed such a revelation of the sin of her heart that Ann spent the rest of the night in earnest supplication for deliverance. The power of prevailing prayer was opened up to her and, like Jacob of old at daybreak, in agony of soul and clinging to God, she exclaimed, "I'll die, but I'll have it." Rising from her knees, she went downstairs where she encountered the young guest who asked the reason for her distress.

"I want to be sanctified throughout—body, soul and spirit," was her reply. He explained that faith in the promises of God would bring the holiness of heart for which she yearned and quoted the verse, "Ask, and it shall be given you; seek, and ye shall find; knock, and it shall be opened unto you."

Again Ann went to her knees, pleading, "Lord, I have been knocking all night. Open unto me! Open unto me!" And Heaven responded to her persevering prayer. At once her mourning was turned into joy and, for two hours, the little house was one of praise. Indeed, it was never again anything else, as Ann walked with God and was led deeper and deeper into the secrets revealed to those who fear Him.

It was at this time that she became known as "Holy Ann," perhaps first called this in derision by some of the boys of the neighborhood. As she realized the true meaning of the name, her prayer was, "Father, they are calling me Holy Ann. Please make me holy, so the children will not be telling lies." Her simple petition found an answer in the fragrance of her humble and faithful Christian witness, permeating the lives of all she met. "Holy Ann" she became to the generation who knew her, and to succeeding ones as well.

Her stories of answers to prayer were numerous. One of the greatest interest is that concerning Dr. Reid's well which always was dry for several months during the summer. His young sons were carrying water from a distance to supply not only family needs but those of the stock as well. One day, as Ann was talking to her charges about a prayer-answering God and telling some of her own experiences, Henry Reid said in a bantering manner, "Ann, why don't you ask your Father to send water in that well, and not have us boys work so hard?"

The question proved to be a direct challenge to her faith. Alone in her own room, she prayed, "Father, You heard what Henry said tonight. If I get up in class-meeting and say, 'My God shall supply all your need according to his riches in glory by Christ Jesus,' the boys won't believe I am what I profess to be, if You don't send the water in the well." Continuing to pray for some time, she received an assurance that her petition had been heard. With the words upon her lips, "Father, if I am what I profess to be, there will be water in the well tomorrow morning," she went to bed and to sound sleep.

The next morning, Henry was preparing for his long walk to draw water for the needs of the day when, to his astonishment, Ann picked up two empty pails and walked to the well that he had remarked was "as dry as the kitchen floor." In a few minutes, she returned to the house and to the watching, incredulous lad, with the same two pails filled to the brim with clear water.

"What do you say now?" was Ann's triumphant query to the surprised boy who, in turn, could only ask, "Why didn't you do that long ago and save us all that work?" Years afterward a friend of Ann's who knew the truth of the incident, said that from that time, the well never was dry again, even in the hottest summer. Who can say that the day of miracles is past?

Ann's long life of ninety-six years was filled with prayer and praise to God for what He had done for her and was able to do for others. Her declining years were spent in the homes of friends who regarded it an honor to minister to her. The Mayor of Toronto assisted at her funeral. The Sunday after her death he remarked, "I have had two honors this week. It has been my privilege to have an interview with the President of the United States. This is a great honor. Then I have been pallbearer to 'Holy Ann'" (Ann Preston). And with no discredit whatever to President Theodore Roosevelt, he added, "Of the two honors, I prize the latter most."

LITTLE THINGS

He was only a lad from Jerusalem,
   Not specially bad—or good.
But straight to the Master he went and said,
   "Here's my little parcel of food.
It isn't much, but it's all I have:
   My mother gave it to me:
The loaves are few, the fishes but two:
   I gladly give them to Thee."
It was only a parcel of food for one,
   But that day it was multiplied.
God has chosen the things that are naught,
   That HE may be glorified.

She was only a humble village maid
   To whom Gabriel came that night;
"Thou art highly favored of God," he said,
   But she trembled at the sight.
"Fear not," he added, "I bring the good news.
   A Son shall be born of thee:
The kingdom of David shall be His right,
   And, Jesus, His name shall be."
She was only a humble village maid
   In whom God had come to abide.
But HE has chosen the things that are naught,
   That HE may be glorified.
              —G.R.H.W.

Isaac Marsden

EARNEST MERCHANT PREACHER

The landlady at Wellington Inn, Doncaster, listened as the twenty-seven year old Isaac regaled the inmates of the bar with the news that he had finished with the old life. She could remember times when this wild, dissolute, infidel ringleader had overturned tables, broken wine glasses, and held the room spellbound with his caricaturing of the latest political speaker or the humble preacher at the Wesleyan Chapel. But he was a good customer, as well as a lodger at the Inn, for his father, a manufacturer of cloth, had rented two rooms. One was used for displaying his bolts of material to customers, the other as a bedroom where either he or his son could stay the night when returning from neighboring fairs or markets.

When Isaac, however, knelt down on the sanded floor, and with terrible earnestness, implored God to save the souls of the young men he had been guilty of leading into vice, her amazement turned to cynicism and laughter. Isaac would soon be back to his old ways!

From childhood, however, there had been good influences thrown around Isaac's life. His had been the good fortune to be born of a pious mother and an industrious father, on June 3, 1807, in Skelmansthorpe, Yorkshire. When his older brother died, Isaac assumed the role of the eldest son of a family of ten. Isaac as a small child was very withdrawn and quiet. He was contented to play within the walls of his own home, with such familiar objects as the bobbins, known to almost every home in South Yorkshire, where looms were heard to be continually clicking as they turned out woolen cloth.

The Wesleyans and Primitives were most active in Southern Yorkshire, but there was as yet no meeting place in the town where the Marsdens lived. Ann Marsden, Isaac's mother, often lamented the fact that she could rarely attend services at the neighboring districts because of the demands of her growing family. She therefore started informal gatherings in her own kitchen which resulted in regular class-meetings.

A revival came to Skelmansthorpe! Isaac, though young, was moved, and had he confided his inner feelings at this time to an adult, he could have been saved years of wasted and wild living. His mother received blessing at this time and became a power for good. Her husband, though outwardly respectable, was irreligious and did not approve of the family's attendance at services.

William Marsden was a man of strong discipline and possessed a shrewd head for business. He cared little how wild Isaac's pranks might be or how mischievous his deeds, if he would only be diligent in school or work. Through considerable self-denial, the boy was kept at school until he was twelve or thirteen, but although the lad learned to write and do some sums, he did not take kindly to student practice. Reading was his delight, and he devoured any book or newspaper available. The companionships formed at school, however, were not helpful to industry or upright conduct, and so Mr. Marsden removed his son and sent him to learn weaving at the loom.

The boy had no notion for work so confined and concentrated; he often ruined the cloth, so the father put him to "cropping," which job he did until he was sixteen or seventeen. Then the expanding business required Isaac, as his father's assistant, to deliver cloth and collect bills. He proved to be very assiduous in making up the parcels, visiting the fairs and markets, and acting as general salesman. This occupation suited the young man very well. With an unusually strong physique, he could work hard all day long, and then revel a good share of the night without feeling any inconvenience the next morning.

Ann Marsden scarcely saw her son now, for he rarely spent an evening at home. Instead, he frequented the inns of the neighborhood where he had been attending the fairs or markets. As a result of his wide range of reading, he possessed a larger store of knowledge than many of his companions who spent the evenings with him in revelry. And so he would keep them amused by impersonating political and religious speakers. His ability to lead the strong and coerce the weak gave him unlimited influence for evil among the youth.

As the mother watched her wayward boy, her almost hourly prayer became: "O God, save my Isaac. He is beyond the reach of every arm but Thine." Relatives and friends abandoned all hope for him; others predicted the gallows eventually for both him and his companions. The mother continued to cling to God for her boy. One night, the flame of ardent desire within her heart moved her to pray on through the night and into the small hours of the morning. At four o'clock, she was assured by an inward witness that her boy would be converted.

Meanwhile, Isaac grew more reckless week by week. His books, written by Paine and Voltaire, were supplemented by everything which he could lay his hands upon of the same infidel nature. But God works by varied means. When the Rev. Robert Aitkin was to preach at Doncaster, the dissolute youth went to hear the notable minister, hoping to discover some peculiarity of the speaker with which to entertain his circle of friends. The afternoon service pulled hard for the man of God. Someone describing that service said, "The word seemed to rebound back into his own bosom. He shook himself, roared like a lion and said: 'I have long heard that Doncaster was the capital of the devil's kingdom, but now I believe it.'"

Returning home after the sermon, Mr. Aitkin gathered the praying folks together to intercede for the evening service. But meantime, Isaac Marsden was smarting under the probing of the Spirit of God. He had never heard a man thunder out the terrors of the law like this one. The speaker seemed to look into his very face as he denounced his identical sins. His refuge of lies and the protective walls of his well-laid arguments crumbled under the anointed words. Numbed, he was impelled to remain behind and enter the inquiry room. When questioned by some Christians why he had taken this step, he could give no answer—a paralysis had seized him for he "thought nothing and felt nothing."

The influence of that sermon was abiding, but although convicted, Isaac did not yet seek earnestly for mercy. In fact, the following week found him on the very back seat at the Love Feast at Skelmansthorpe with paper and pencil in hand, intending to list the names of the speakers and outline the substance of their talks, parodying it at the Inn. The people were having a joyful time, and he was having work to fill in the notes. His own mother arose and related how she had been praying for her wayward son.

Suddenly the Spirit of the Lord again smote the young man with feelings of remorse:

> "Isaac," He seemed to say, "you have known these people all your life. In sickness and in health, in prosperity and adversity, they have been true to their principles. Some of them have endured persecution for Christ's sake and yet they have honorably maintained their profession. You never knew any of them do a mean, shabby, dishonest deed. They have never told you a lie or tried to deceive you. Are they lying now, or are they speaking the truth? If they are speaking the truth, you are on the wrong side of the hedge."[1]

Like a flash, the young man's infidel arguments appeared hollow and worthless. He could not resist such outstanding evidence. He folded away his notebook and, springing to his feet, told them that their happiness had convicted him. He stated how he was most unhappy, and how he had resolved that if there was a Heaven, he would gain it, and if there was a Hell, he would shun it. Then, with great emphasis, he brought down those unusually long arms of his like a sledgehammer upon the pew door, saying, "And if ever I do get converted, the devil may look out."

The communicants did not know how to receive this information. Was it another practical joke? But the stricken young man knew within his own heart that his life was going to be very different. At the Doncaster Love Feast the next week, he made a similar statement of his intentions. In after years, Mr. Marsden spoke of these public utterances as important milestones in his life.

Now at Doncaster there were four holy men of God of varying ages: young Butler, a tailor, who had been meeting in class-meeting; Rev. William Naylor, a mild and gentle spirit; Friend Unsworth, a pious shoemaker, and Friend Waring, an elderly man noted for piety and wisdom. These four made Isaac their special care, taking him to every meeting, both in the church and in their own homes.

The great crisis of the new birth was reached one Sunday morning, October 11, 1834. Isaac had attended the early six o'clock prayer-meeting, and there he had requested his friends to pray for him every hour of the day, for he meant to do business with God. He had seen himself the vilest of sinners, not only wasting ten precious years of his own life, but being the ringleader for the devil among young men. God forgave him out of His boundless mercy, and it was alone in his own room that the Spirit witnessed to his acceptance with God.

The first act of this prodigal was to return home and report to his mother all that had happened. Ann Marsden turned pale and almost fainted, but she was a bit skeptical. However, the change in her son's conduct soon caused her to rejoice, for she observed that he now spent evenings at home when he would retire to his own room alone. With an open Bible on the chair before him, he would study the Book with delight, meditating and praying. At times he would go to one of his friends for further instruction, but immediately afterwards he would retire for quiet and further study. He had always been a reader, but now it was one Book that enthralled him.

The story of his conversion spread abroad like wild fire. At fairs and markets it became the latest bit of gossip. Peals of laughter would be occasioned, as some who had known him before, looked forward to his next impersonating performance. His four friends knew, however, that the young man was in earnest, and that the devil would use every known device to lure him back. So they impressed upon the new convert that his safety lay in being out and out for God. He must carry war into the very camp of the devil where before he had aided and abetted evil.

Isaac, taking their advice, would mount the wagon after selling his bolts of material, and use it as a preaching stance. When Feast Day came to his town, he would take up position between two drinking houses, witnessing to the merrymakers. At the Doncaster Race Course, he placarded trees and fences with signs. In the Inns where he must needs meet his customers and receive payments, the former reveler would ask for a glass of pure water, paying the price that a glass of beer would cost. He would then hold his temperance lecture, and with it intermingle the Gospel.

Meanwhile, Isaac observed that his four godly friends, possessing the blessing of entire sanctification, preached it, lived it and enforced it. They now impressed upon Isaac "that he could never have the power of learning, or culture, or wealth, or social position, but he might have the power of goodness." They enjoined him to meet with them at every means of grace possible. They pointed out Scriptural commands such as "Be ye holy, for I am holy." They gathered early in the morning before he left for his week's rounds, and would be present to pray with him upon his return on Saturday. An agreement had been reached between them to pray for one another seven times daily.

Isaac, though endeavoring to subdue his strong passions and tempers by praying without ceasing, still had not attained to this blessing of "Perfect Love" which his four good friends still urged upon him whenever they met. Sixteen months after his conversion, the seeker found his heart's cry answered. He writes:

> I first dared to give God my whole heart, and believed that the blood of Jesus Christ cleansed me from all sin. This happened at a place called Langworth, at the Inn where I put up. Before I lay down to rest, I made a practice of reading a portion of Scripture on my knees, and I did the same in the morning. In this way I had read twice and a half through the Bible, and, as I got to prayer, this passage came into mind: "My son, give Me thine heart." And I said to God: "Here, Lord, Thou shalt have it," believing that a God so pure and holy would not keep sin in His hand. And, blessed be God! I still feel that the blood of Jesus Christ cleanseth me from all sin. O my God, may this ever be my experience! [2]

Towards the latter end of 1836, Mr. Marsden was called to preach and placed on the Methodist plan. He had already been faithfully witnessing and seeing friends and customers brought to God. But it was with some difficulty that he could adjust to the orthodox behavior demanded in the pulpit. He, in fact, never did fully conform, but often scattered to the winds everything that would restrict his freedom. Sedate Christians had reason to complain of these innovations, but he felt men were perishing from lack of the Gospel, and the sentiments of his heart are expressed in his journal. "O may the Lord ever be with me and make me in earnest!" he writes. "God is in earnest—Heaven is in earnest—devils are in earnest—Hell is in earnest. And in order to save my soul and them that hear me, I must be in earnest, or be in danger of being damned in the pulpit. Souls are on the verge of Hell. We must be in earnest to pluck them as brands from eternal burnings." [3]

His journal entries if 1838 reveal the same sentiments:

> May God help me to live this year to His honor and glory as I never did. I feel determined by God's help to spend and be spent in His service. I feel daily His blood cleanses me from all sin. My evidence is brighter than ever. What thousands there are in the Church that live without this blessing! O my God, arouse the Church to seek after all its privileges. Mr. Harris says: "So long have we accustomed ourselves to be content with little things that we have gone far in disqualifying ourselves for the reception of great things." O my God open mine eyes to behold all my privileges. Give my soul an impulse and raise me nearer to Thy Throne. I want a spiritual earthquake to take place in my soul every day. [4]

> We are languid in our prayers when we ought to be inspired. What we have expected is only our feebleness. There is too much sameness and oneness amongst us. We go to preach, we go to hear, we go to class-meeting, we go to prayer-meeting, and we expect no good. We go to work like an old man eighty years of age to break stones on a cold winter's day. [5]

> Sink me to the lowest depths and raise me up to the highest privileges of religious experience. O for an earnest of the Spirit of power and of glory! Revive me every moment. Enable me to live like some immortal being let down from Thy Throne. Make me a stranger to the fear of man, and help me to carry with me an atmosphere of salvation. Lord, Lord, lead Thy ignorant, unworthy creature, every breath, thought, word, feeling, action, day, night, hour, moment, and Thou shalt have the praise. [6]

As a preacher, Mr. Marsden was mighty. He could not tolerate the stillness of death and formality in his audience. In the middle of some discourse, he would stop and make some pronouncement which would startle his hearers into thoughtfulness. He wanted to make them think. It was little wonder that the more wealthy and respectable should resent his unvarnished plainness. They accused him of being mad, and a lie was circulated to the effect that he had committed suicide. It was believed by many until he turned up to prove it to be a lie.

During seventeen years he preached 3,370 sermons in Yorkshire, Nottinghamshire, Lincolnshire, and Lancashire where God signally owned his labors with hundreds of souls being brought into the Kingdom. At Wigan, he was particularly assisted and revival ensued. Whenever an enlivened church wished to make attack upon some evil den of iniquity, some public house, some notorious part of town, they called Isaac Marsden to help.

He was exceptionally gifted in personal work, and would often dismount to speak with a stone-breaker, ditch-digger, or passerby, often kneeling down and praying for their salvation. When entering upon a series of services in a new district, he would first appeal to leaders and members to fully consecrate themselves to God. Like a soldier, he would reconnoiter before attack. He would stroll through the town, noting its salient points and its weaknesses. Each stranger he met would be accosted, invited to the services, and given a tract. On Sunday evening after the service, the public houses and shops that were open would be visited by this ardent fisher of men who would often kneel down to pray, and invite the customers to the services.

"Can you tell me which house the Lord Jesus lives in?" he would ask of a stranger in order to strike up a conversation, and he would leave the people thinking.

If the church in which he spoke had only professed Christians attending, he would proceed very decorously with his sermon, and then suddenly he would close his Bible, and announce: "The devil is in the chapel. I can't preach. Let us pray." He would then pour out his heart with a torrent of words that revealed his burden for the man that was not there—or was he? The Sabbath-breaker, the profligate, the drunkard, the thief, were interceded for until the congregation would tremble. At the evening service, the place of worship would be well filled with people unaccustomed to regular churchgoing. The respectable members would not understand his stratagem, but his unusual methods attracted sinners into the house of God.

Isaac Marsden possessed a prophetic insight as did many of the early itinerant preachers. They exercised gifts of the Spirit for their ministry, when scarcely aware of such possession! This man of God lived so near Heaven in prayer that he often caught the slightest whispers of the Spirit. His warnings to rebellious sinners, frequently uttered before the congregation, were often fulfilled to the letter. In public prayer, he would supplicate for the needs of individuals in such a way as to astound the listener who knew that such details could scarcely be known by a stranger save that "the secret of the Lord" was with him, and that the Lord revealeth His secrets unto His servants.

Small children were never neglected in his ministrations. He often instituted orange, apple, or bun feasts and invited them along to his meetings to sing hallelujah. Many of these grew up to be honored ministers and useful workers who owed their first impressions of the Gospel to his fatherly and loving manner. William Booth was only fourteen when he heard this passionate pleader and Isaac Marsden claimed him as one of his lambs. Thereafter the work of the Salvation Army was followed with profound heart interest.

The claims of the churches became excessive as he became more recognized as a powerful preacher. As a result, his business began to suffer. He was faced with the question, "Shall I attend to business and make a fortune, or let business decline and give myself to evangelism?" In a journal entry, May 11, 1846, he notes:

> If the Lord ever puts me in such a position that I can give up business, I promise this day by His help that I will lay down the world, and take up His Gospel, and preach it till death. Lord help me. Thou knowest the weakness of man, and covenants are of no avail without divine aid. Make me faithful to Thy cause in every calling in life.[7]

All through these years, Isaac Marsden was a devoted son to his mother who had delicate health and suffered acutely. Before leaving on a journey, he always entered her sick room and prayed earnestly that she would be sustained during his absence. Upon returning, he would rush into her bedroom and kneeling down, thank God that she was still alive. Here at her side, he would plead with God for hours. Her life ended in peace and triumph in 1847. He insisted upon preaching her funeral sermon as he felt no one else could do justice to her saintly life.

On one of his preaching journeys, he had met the daughter of a respectable farmer and a mutual affection sprang up between them. Because Mr. Marsden still held responsibility as head of his family and she must consider her father's welfare, it was not for another seven years that they could consider marriage. Isaac Marsden was now forty-seven years of age.

Mary Barker was in every way suited to be a helpmeet for her husband. Though opposite in so many ways, they supplied to each other the very qualities they needed. She was a class-leader and successful worker in the church. Rarely did this devoted couple spend Sundays together from one year's end to another. And most evenings as well were occupied in taking preaching appointments, but the wife had willingly agreed that their union should in no wise hinder Isaac's fulfilling God's call. His schedule was never altered for loved companionship with the woman of his choice.

Shortly after his marriage, his financial circumstances were such that he could now, by transferring it to other members of the family, sever his connection with his father's business.

As this man of God neared the end of his labors, how did he view the experience he had received in his late twenties?

I feel a settled conviction of the necessity of a full salvation always, especially for pulpit work and the permanent revival of the churches. The Church has for a long time been going down to the world, until the distinction has been nearly lost. The birthday of the Church was the day of Pentecost—the festival of the Holy Ghost. It is not the external form and custom, but the Holy Ghost that makes the Church really Christian. He is the soul that fills and animates her, and combines all her individual members into the unity of one body.[8]

What is to be done to raise Methodism? My answer is: only one thing for the pulpit and the pew, not a splendid ritual, nor splendid chapels, nor splendid sermons, nor splendid concerts, nor splendid lectures, nor bazaars. The Pentecost is that one thing for pulpit and pew. All other things without this are splendid sins, and splendid professions, and splendid shams.[9]

The long and frequent journeys, occasioning exposure to inclement weather, weakened the robust frame. He began to feel a languor that took his appetite and rest. His wife tenderly nursed him during those long nights of sickness, as he lay like a lamb, feeling that his tempestuous mission was almost finished. He said one day, "I don't feel anything or think anything of Isaac Marsden; it is all Christ. . . . I have been looking back and reviewing seventy years, but I see nothing but the Atonement!—the Atonement at every turn!"[10]

On January 17, 1882, at seventy-five years of age, the militant spirit of Isaac Marsden joined the Church triumphant. The warrior preacher had utilized every ransomed power for the extension of God's kingdom.

How did Mr. Marsden maintain the experience through those long years, and keep unabated that zeal and vision for the lost? The secret was to be found in his prayer closet. Seven times a day this man sought the face of the Lord, although his intimates never knew of this practice. "He literally prayed without ceasing," says his biographer. He hated anything like frivolity or foolish conversation, gossip or slander.

"I have no liking for dinner-parties," he stated. "I can do with a chat at tea, and then be free and easy, but as soon as breakfast is over, I long to be off into my room to my books and papers. Life is short, and I feel I have not five minutes to spare."

As a new convert, Isaac Marsden had set up the chair within the bedroom for Bible study and prayer, and now, as an aged warrior, he had not ceased to keep this quiet tryst with Christ although the demands of the church had lain heavily upon him.

QUOTATIONS BY ISAAC MARSDEN

Shall we then be counted among the dead men? O no! We must be counted among the living—among the higher-life men. A man of real life will look alive and speak a living language. His prayers will have fire enshrined in them and will have wings of fire, which will rise to Heaven and return with answers before he rises from his knees. But the wings of a dead man's prayers are of ice, which will freeze him fast under the wings of death.[11]

. . . For this the world will call us "mad." There is not only a "mad zeal" in serving Christ and in carrying men out of themselves, but there is a worse kind of madness—lukewarmness, supineness, and disbelief. Many read that Christ was born in a stable and laid in a manger, but they never go to see Him. If they could read that He was born in a palace, there would be cheap trips to the place, and the rich would go and offer their gifts. But Christianity remains unaltered. It never adapts itself to foolish notions or false theories.[12]

Unbelief is the blue mold that grows on idle and lazy souls. Keep with duty, always working with Christ, and then Jesus will take care that His bride walks with Him "in white." Never belong to those who say, "I cannot," "I am unworthy," "I had rather not"; but up and at it. Let it be always a settled thing in your own mind that you are unworthy, but don't talk about it. Talking much about it is either canting pride or canting hypocrisy. Be a noble soul. You are unworthy, but your Jesus is worthy—and worthy of you. You are weak, but He is strong. Let Him be your Alpha and Omega—your all in all.[13]

Alfred Cookman

WASHED IN THE BLOOD OF THE LAMB

"Sweep a circle of three feet around the cross of Jesus, and you take in all that there was of Alfred Cookman," wrote De Witt Talmage after the death of this good man. It had not always been so with this talented but devoted minister. When only twenty years of age, Alfred Cookman had suffered serious spiritual loss while attending a ministerial conference by engaging in foolish and trifling conversation. This forfeiture of abounding grace he sustained for ten long years, but the lessons learned by such failure were the means God employed in shaping this average Christian into a veritable saint who henceforth inscribed over his hands, his feet, his lips—"Sacred to Jesus."

His father, George Cookman, a Yorkshireman, was converted at eighteen years of age. While undertaking a business engagement which took him across to America, he received a clear call from God to return to that land as a preacher of the Gospel. After spending a time in that country, he returned to Britain for his bride, Sarah Barton, whose home was in Doncaster. As a new convert, she had demonstrated her fidelity to her new-found faith in the way in which she had endured persecution at the hands of her aunt within her own home. She gladly left her affluent circumstances to courageously venture forth with her husband, in February 1827, to share the hardships of the new country.

Alfred was born in Columbia, Pennsylvania, in January 1828. The consciousness of his parents in regard to their spiritual responsibility resulted in their giving the oldest of their six children to God in a special way. He never forgot his godly heritage as he writes years later:

> I shall never cease to be grateful for the instruction and example of a faithful father and an affectionate mother. I cannot call up a period in my life, even in my earliest childhood, when I had not

the fear of God before my eyes. When about seven years of age, I persuaded my parents to let me attend a watch-night service. My father preached on the Second Coming of Christ. Thinking that perhaps the end of the world was just at hand, I realized for the first time my unpreparedness for the trying scenes of the Judgment and trembled at the prospect. I date my awakening from that time.[1]

As a lad of eleven, Alfred attended one of his father's services where the penitent form was crowded with seekers. His heart, too, was moved upon by the Holy Spirit. As there seemed no room for him at the front, he made his way to a corner of the church. Here, the earnest prayer of the weeping boy was, "Precious Savior, Thou art saving others, oh, wilt Thou not save me?" He afterwards related his experience at that time:

> As I wept and prayed and struggled, a kind hand was laid on my head. I opened my eyes and found it was a Mr. James Hamilton, prominent member and elder in the Presbyterian Church. He had observed my interest and, obeying the promptings of a kind, sympathizing Christian heart, he came to encourage and help me. I remember how sweetly he unfolded the nature of faith and the plan of salvation. I said, "I will believe, I do believe, I now believe that Jesus is my Savior, that He saves me, yes, even now," and immediately
>
>> "The opening heavens did round me shine
>> With beams of sacred bliss;
>> And Jesus showed His mercy mine
>> And whispered I am His."[2]

With the incoming of spiritual life, Alfred yearned, though so young, to help others and commenced a prayer service for lads his own age, several of whom were converted.

The same year, his father was appointed to Wesley Chapel in Washington D.C., from which post he also was elected to serve as chaplain to the United States Senate. In 1841, he felt it his duty to visit his aged father, Alfred's grandfather, in England. Alfred was asked if he should like to accompany him but, feeling a responsibility to his mother and the younger members of the family during his father's absence, he declined. Mr. Cookman sailed from New York for Liverpool, but the vessel did not reach its destination, and its fate never was determined. The tragedy, almost overwhelming in its effects upon the now widowed Mrs. Cookman, brought out the best in Alfred's character. Manfully and bravely he attempted to take his father's place, and his mother remarked that eternity alone would reveal all that he was as a son and brother to the bereaved family.

The death of the husband and father necessitated a change of residence, and the city of Baltimore became the site of the Cookman home. Before he was fifteen, Alfred became a Sunday School teacher. The next year, he joined several other young men in the organization of a mission to sailors and poor children who frequented the docks of the harbor on Chesapeake Bay. They rented a room which they named "The City Bethel," and there they conducted services.

Alfred, though the youngest member of the group, so clearly demonstrated his ability as a speaker as well as the divine touch upon his life, that friends began to recognize his ultimate call of God to the ministry. His first effort of note in this direction was the delivery of a funeral sermon at the death of a Christian friend, when he chose as his text, "To die is gain."

So it was that at eighteen years of age, Alfred Cookman said good-bye to his family and entered upon his ministerial career. Among his mother's parting words to him was the exhortation, "My son, if you would be supremely happy or extensively useful in your ministry, you must be an entirely sanctified servant of Jesus." This admonition made the most profound impression upon his mind and heart. He states:

> Frequently I felt led to yield myself to God and pray for the grace of an entire sanctification. But then the experience would lift itself up, in my view, as a mountain of glory, and I would say, "It is not for me. I could not possibly scale that shining summit. And if I could, my besetments and trials are such, I could not successfully maintain so lofty a position."[3]

His itinerary took him to various preaching appointments and, at one of these, his heart was gladdened by the arrival of Bishop and

Mrs. Hamline for the purpose of dedicating a new church. This saintly man remained about a week, preaching several times with the unction of the Holy Spirit. He also conversed with Alfred in a pointed way regarding his need of sanctification. His exhortations had a most beneficial effect upon the young minister and drove him to earnest prayer. He describes what happened in his own words:

> Kneeling by myself, I brought an entire consecration to Christ. . . . I covenanted with my own heart and with my heavenly Father that this entire but unworthy offering should remain upon the altar, and that henceforth I would please God by believing that the altar (Christ) sanctifieth the gift. Do you ask what was the immediate effect? I answer, peace—a broad, deep, full, satisfying and sacred peace. This proceeded not only from the testimony of a good conscience before God, but likewise from the presence and operation of the Spirit in my heart. Still I could not say that I was entirely sanctified, except as I had sanctified or set apart myself unto God.

> The day following, finding Bishop and Mrs. Hamline, I ventured to tell them of my consecration and faith in Jesus, and in the confession I realized increasing light and strength. A little while after, it was proposed by Mrs. Hamline that we spend a season in prayer. Prostrated before God, one and another prayed While I was thus engaged, God, for Christ's sake, gave me the Holy Spirit as I had never received Him before, so that I was constrained to conclude and confess:

> "Tis done! Thou dost this moment save,
> With full salvation bless;
> Redemption through Thy blood I have,
> And spotless love and peace."

> The great work of sanctification that I had so often prayed and hoped for was wrought in me, even in me. I could not doubt it. The evidence in my case was as direct and indubitable as the witness of sonship received at the time of my adoption into the family of Heaven. Oh, it was glorious, divinely glorious!

> Need I say that the experience of sanctification inaugurated a new epoch in my religious life? Oh, what blessed rest in Jesus! Oh, what an abiding experience of purity through the blood of the Lamb! What a conscious union and constant communion with God! What increased power to do or suffer the will of my Father in Heaven! What delight in the Master's service! What fear to grieve the infi-

nitely Holy Spirit! What love for, and desire to be with, the entirely
sanctified! What joy in religious conversation! What confidence in
prayer! What illumination in the perusal of the sacred Word! What
increased unction in the performance of public duties![4]

But this sacred experience was marred when Cookman, present
at his first conference of the Methodist Church, engaged with other
ministers in conversation which quenched the Holy Spirit. He said
later:

> Forgetting how easily the infinitely Holy Spirit might be grieved,
> I allowed myself to drift into the spirit of the hour. And after an
> indulgence in foolish joking and story-telling, I realized that I had
> suffered serious loss. To my next field of labor, I proceeded with
> consciously diminished power.
>
> Perhaps to satisfy my conscience, I began to favor the argu-
> ments of those who insisted that sanctification, as a work of the
> Holy Spirit, could not involve an experience distinct from regenera-
> tion.[5]

Although the young minister no longer had the inward assurance of full salvation, his preaching during the next decade seemed
most acceptable to the churches he pastored. He was the most popular preacher in the Conference and was in demand on many plat-
forms. Calls came from churches in the larger cities in rapid succession. But in spite of all the outward success, he was dissatisfied and
realized that nothing could surpass personal godliness. Admonish-
ing his younger brother who was contemplating entering the ministry, he wrote:

> Let no idle, no secret sin, no unwillingness to toil or sacrifice
> or suffer, debar you from the full realization of your privileges in
> the Gospel of God's dear Son. However imperfect your mental
> and physical developments may seem to yourself there is no reason
> why, as a Christian, you should not rival a Fletcher, a McCheyne, a
> Summerfield, in their almost seraphic purity, zeal, and devotion.
> Attend, then, to the all-important subject of personal piety in the
> first instance, and I have no fear for the rest.[6]

It was during the 1857 revival that swept across the American continent, that Alfred Cookman was challenged to retake his stand in defense of the doctrine of "Perfect Love." He was pastoring at this time the church at Green Street, Philadelphia, and had come to acknowledge that much of his energy had been frittered away by the inner conflict that had raged within. The Spirit was leading him back to the simple faith of his first consecration, but was also directing him forward to a more mature understanding of the doctrine and experience. Of his restoration, he wrote ten years after:

> Oh, how many precious years I wasted in quibbling and debating respecting theological differences, not seeing that I was antagonizing a doctrine that must be spiritually discerned, and the tendency of which is manifestly to bring people nearer to God!
>
> Meanwhile, I had foolishly fallen into the habit of using tobacco, an indulgence which, besides the palatable gratification, seemed to minister to both my nervous and social nature. Years elapsed. When I would confront the obligation of entire consecration, the sacrifice of my foolish habit would be presented as a test of obedience. I would consent. Light, strength and blessing were the result.
>
> Afterward, temptation would be presented. I would listen to suggestions like these: "This is one of the good things of God." "Your religion does not require a course of asceticism." "This indulgence is not especially forbidden on the New Testament page." "Some good people whom you know are addicted to this practice." Thus, seeking to quiet an uneasy conscience, I would drift back into the old habit again.
>
> After a while, I began to see that the indulgence at best was doubtful for me, and that I was giving my carnality rather than my Christian experience the benefit of the doubt. It could not really harm me to give it up, while to persist in the practice was costing me too much in my religious enjoyments.
>
> I found that after all my objections to sanctification as a distinct work of grace, there was nevertheless a conscious lack in my own religious experience—it was not strong, round, full, abiding. I frequently asked myself, "What is it that I need and desire in comparison with what I have and profess?"

I looked at the three steps insisted upon by the friends of holiness—namely: "First, entire consecration; second, acceptance of Jesus moment by moment as a perfect Savior; third, a meek and definite profession of the grace received," and I said, "These are scriptural and reasonable duties. . . . I will cast aside all preconceived theories, doubtful indulgences, and culpable unbelief, and retrace my steps." Alas that I should have wandered from the light at all, and afterward wasted so many years in vacillating between self and God! Can I ever forgive myself? Oh, what bitter, bitter memories!

The acknowledgment I make is constrained by candor and a concern for others. It is the greatest humiliation of my life. If I had the ear of those who have entered into the clearer light of Christian purity, I would beseech and charge them with a brother's interest and earnestness that they be warned by my folly. Oh, let such consent to die, if it were possible, ten deaths before they willfully depart from the path of holiness, for, if they retrace their steps, there will still be the remembrance of original purity tarnished, and that will prove a drop of bitterness in the cup of their sweetest comfort. . . .

I again accepted Christ as my Savior from all sin, realized the witness of the same Spirit, and since then have been walking in the light—realizing that experimental doctrine of the fellowship and communion with saints. I humbly and gratefully testify that the blood of Jesus cleanseth me from all sin.

"As ye have therefore received Christ Jesus the Lord, so walk ye in Him." That is, as I understand, "Maintain the same attitude before God you assumed when you accepted Christ as your all-sufficient Savior." I received Him in a spirit of entire consecration, implicit faith, and humble confession. The constant repetition of these three steps, I find, enables me to walk in Him. I cannot afford for a single moment ever to remove my offering, to fail in looking unto Jesus, or to part with the spirit of confession.[7]

In 1851, Rev. Cookman was married to Annie Bruner. The union was a happy one, based, as Alfred remarked on the tenth anniversary of their wedding, upon the "stones" of love, truth, purity, kindness, fidelity, sincerity, constancy, thankfulness, holiness, and Christ as the Foundation.

Notwithstanding constant religious and evangelistic activities of most strenuous nature, Alfred Cookman was basically a family man.

He took the utmost delight in his nine children. His letters to them during his enforced absences are full of fatherly affection and admonitions directed to their spiritual good. Two of them preceded him in death—a sweet baby girl, Rebecca, and his firstborn son, Bruner, in his sixteenth year. To the great comfort of his parents, the lad had been a consistent Christian from the time of his conversion at ten years of age. Cookman regarded Bruner's life as a "temporary loan" which "made earth more beautiful, Heaven more attractive."

His speaking appointments necessitated absences from his loved partner. Once when his loneliness almost overwhelmed him, he wrote to her:

> I bowed my knee in prayer and sweetly realized that I was in the best of company. My compassionate Savior came quickly to my relief, and the room was transformed into the audience-chamber of Deity. Oh, how unutterably sweet—how indescribably valuable, is the religion of the Lord Jesus! [8]

This unusual man received his strength at the Mercy Seat. His wife tells how she would remonstrate with him about his night vigils only to receive the answer that he could not rest while the burden of the people was upon him. Often he would wrestle in his study until the day broke. This intimate communion with the Lord affected his public prayers. One man in a service, hearing his impassioned pleading, opened his eyes to see the minister kneeling with hands stretched toward Heaven, and then rising from his knees and reaching as high as he could. Then falling upon his knees again, he thanked God for the blessings asked for.

An intelligent young convert was impressed by the godly Alfred Cookman. "What sermon did you hear him preach?" he was asked. "I have never heard him preach, but I have watched him as he was walking along the street," was the answer.

Living as he did amid the struggles of the nation in regard to the great issues of secession and slavery, Cookman could not remain a silent onlooker. Before the breaking out of the Civil War, he delivered an antislavery sermon from Isa. 8:12, 13, "Say ye not, a confederacy, to all them to whom this people shall say, a confederacy; neither fear ye their fear, nor be afraid. Sanctify the Lord of hosts himself; and let him be your fear, and let him be your dread." As he spoke, his face shone with a heavenly light, and his words were surcharged with divine emphasis and power.

During the conflict that ensued, he served the Christian Commission at the front, not only in a temporal way by alleviating the physical misery of the soldiers, but also by the distribution of Bibles and tracts and by preaching and personal visitation.

It is not strange that Cookman's arduous public life took a heavy toll of his strength. Instead of taking holidays, he would engage in strenuous efforts at some camp-meeting. Although he felt his physical powers waning, he did not refuse any opportunity to lift his voice like a trumpet in behalf of the full Gospel. On October 22, 1871, he preached his last sermon. Announcing his subject and holding a faded leaf in his hand, he solemnly read the text, "We all do fade as a leaf" (Isa. 64: 6). The congregation remarked afterward upon the unusual brightness emanating from his countenance. As he finished the address, he handed the leaf to a friend with the words, "The leaf and the preacher are very much alike—fading."

He was so weak that two friends escorted him homeward, and he remarked to them: "I know it is not popular to hold up the doctrine of holiness, but I thought I would do my whole duty then; I feel this may be my last opportunity."[9]

Among his final utterances were: "I am sweeping through the gates," and "washed in the blood of the Lamb." God gave this loving child of His, who spent only forty-four years in this vale of tears, such a glimpse of the efficacy of the cleansing of the "blood of the Lamb who was slain" as seems to be granted to few on this earth. But this affirmation was more than a once-uttered act of witness. It was the theme of his sick room; it created the atmosphere that gathered in that sacred place.

Doubtless the same reality that caused the martyrs to sing in the flames, enabled the suffering preacher to exult in the fruits of Redemption as they applied to the vital needs of the hour. His feet were painful in the extreme because of a peculiarly violent form of rheumatism. He explained that if every bone in his ankles and the soles of his feet were a tooth, with the raw nerves throbbing acutely in each, it would be comparable to the pain he endured. But to him it was turned to blessing. Let us listen as he explains:

> I have known for many years what it is to be washed in the blood of the Lamb; now I understand the full meaning of that verse, "These are they which came out of great tribulation, and have washed their robes, and made them white in the blood of the Lamb." I used to maintain that the blood was sufficient, but I am coming to know that tribulation brings us to the blood that cleanseth.[10]

When his mother had reminded him that the blessed Savior had suffered in His feet, he commented, "You know the nails pierced His precious feet, and He can sympathize with me in my sufferings."

Mr. Cookman had a vision of Heaven during his final illness. He declared it to have been more than a dream. He found himself just inside the gates and was first greeted by his grandfather who said, "When you were in England, I took great pleasure in showing you the different places of interest; now I welcome you to Heaven, my grandson, washed in the blood of the Lamb!" He was next received by his father, whose features were as distinct to him as they had ever been during his boyhood. The greeting was on the same note, "Welcome, my son, washed in the blood of the Lamb!" Then his brother George embraced him exclaiming, "Welcome, my brother, washed in the blood of the Lamb!" And lastly his son Bruner repeated the refrain, "Welcome, my father, washed in the blood of the Lamb." Each one of these in turn presented him to the Throne. Alfred's comment to his wife was: "That was abundant entrance."

Hear this advocate of cleansing through the blood proclaiming once more the same message:

> The best hours of my illness were when the fierce fires of suffering were kindling and scorching all around me. It has convinced me that full salvation is the only preparation for the ten thousand contingencies that belong to a mortal career. Oh, how soothing to feel, hour by hour, that the soul has been washed in the blood

of the Lamb, and to experience the inspiration of that perfect love that casteth out fear that hath torment.[11]

And so as the end approached, the same witness was given to all! To his physician it was: "Washed in the blood of the Lamb." To a Presbyterian minister he confessed to the assurance of full salvation, saying, "Such views of Christ's presence with me—such views of His cleansing blood have I had never before!" To a dear colleague in the ministry, he said, "I have tried to preach Holiness; I have honestly declared it; and oh, what a comfort it is to me now! I have been true to Holiness, and now Jesus saves me—saves me fully. I am so sweetly washed in the blood of the Lamb." And to his brother, just before the end, it was, "Death is the gate to endless glory; I am washed in the blood of the Lamb." Another loved one just heard him whisper, "This is the sickest day of my life, but all is well; I am so glad I have preached full salvation; what should I do without it now? If you forget everything else, remember my testimony, 'Washed in the blood of the Lamb.'"[12]

And so he passed through "the gates," November 12, 1871, to join that great throng who are "washed in the blood of the Lamb."

The words of Bishop Foster at Mr. Cookman's funeral service could well have been voiced by many another, "The most sacred man I have ever known is he who is enshrined in that casket."

QUOTATIONS BY ALFRED COOKMAN

Christians never part for the last time! We separate, but it is as the angels do, going forth for the performance of the Divine will, but with the assurance that our home is before the Throne. Thank God, we belong to a sky-born, sky-guided, sky-returning race, and sweetly the peace-march beats, "Home, brothers, home!"

Unction is that subtle, intangible, irresistible influence of the Holy Spirit that seals instruction upon the hearts to which it is given. It is not the eloquent men of this world, the orators of great occasions, whose words linger longest in their influence upon the hearts of men. The unction may oftentimes be rather in the utterances of a humble disciple than in the delivery of a powerful sermon. For this I am more concerned than for anything else.[13]

Let us be a holy people. Holiness is power. What the Church needs, what the world around is looking and waiting for, is more of power. We must have it for the fulfillment of our high and holy mission, viz., the spiritual conquest of the world.

Elizabeth Baxter

CHRISTIAN "HERALDESS"

In the pleasant vale of Evesham through which the Avon flows, the birth of a daughter, Elizabeth, on December 16, 1837, gladdened the hearts of Thomas and Edith Foster. Little could they realize, as they looked at this small bundle of life, that she was destined to affect multitudes. For Elizabeth Foster Baxter became co-editor of the *Christian Herald* and, through her devoted Christian life and ministry in pen and word, brought salvation, holiness, and healing to many.

Elizabeth had much to be grateful for in her father's Quaker background of sturdy faith and principle. Her mother was an ardent member of the Church of England and, in its atmosphere, the child was reared and trained. Into the home on High Street, in times of election, would come the Liberal Candidate. The little lass would silently repose under the table listening to the fortunes of parliamentary battle.

Of the religious influences of her home, she said:

> Born of God-fearing parents who strictly observed the Lord's Day and family prayers, I was nevertheless very ignorant of divine things. . . . Like other children belonging to the Church of England, I was taught the Church Catechism, and again and again I pondered over the words that in baptism I was "made a member of Christ, a child of God and an inheritor of the kingdom of Heaven." I could not tell what that meant, but I knew, if it meant anything, it must mean having to do with God, that there was a real something which I was sure had not taken place in me.
>
> And then I became much occupied with the promises made to God in my name by my godfather and godmother that I should "renounce the devil and all his works, the vain pomp and glory of this world, with all covetous desires of the same, and the carnal desires of the flesh, so that thou wilt not follow, nor be led by them."

What did this mean? It was a matter of supreme moment to me to know what I was let in for, how far I was personally responsible.[1]

After a confirmation class, Elizabeth remained behind to ask the Vicar if, before she was confirmed, she was responsible for these promises. A hurried "Good morning," as he took his leave, left her half bitter. The same question was put to two other clergymen, neither of whom gave a satisfactory answer. So she said, "The question remained unsolved, and I remained unsaved."

A governess was employed to instruct Elizabeth until she was eleven years of age. Then, for five years, she attended a boarding-school at Worcester. During this time, she made good resolutions and practiced much self-control. She read her Bible, but it did not speak to her as she would have liked. Nor did she ever meet with anyone who could tell her how the boundless grace of God can swallow up her sin. Her own words describe this difficult period in her life:

> To the world, I was a gay, thoughtless girl, but often I would get alone for hours together and cry to God to help me, with no clear idea of how help was to come. It was not sorrow for sin. I had not any particular sins on my conscience, but a general sense of being all wrong, more like a "fearful looking for of judgment and fiery indignation." On the other hand, I had a certain faith that God is love. If I could only have seen how His just wrath for sin could be reconciled with His love, I could have been at peace. My only idea of the sacrifice of Christ was that He died a martyr of His own holy life of love, which was misunderstood of men.[2]

The passing of her father, when she was only eighteen, affected her deeply. She had loved him as she loved no one else on earth. At his grave, she vowed she would gladly yield up her seeing or hearing, if she could only know how sin could be put away. After his death, she spent some time with an uncle who was a vicar in Suffolk. While there, she visited a dying girl who asked, "Miss Foster, do you know the way?"

She could only answer, "I would give all the world if I had it, to know the way. But, if I may shut the door, I think I can pray to God for both of us, that He will show us the way." She then prayed, asking that they both might be shown the path to God's salvation.

Within a short time, the dying girl sent her friend the message, "Tell Miss Foster that I have found the way." Elizabeth's unsatisfied heart experienced something akin to jealousy, and gladly would she have changed places with her. As she watched the funeral procession from the window, her aching heart caused her to sigh, "Oh, God, show me also the way to find Thee!"

Her prayer was answered through a former school friend, Caroline Smith, who had also lost her father and wished to comfort Elizabeth in her loss. She herself had been shown the way to Christ through Rev. Robert Aitken of Pendeen. Caroline opened the Bible at Isaiah 53: 6: "All we like sheep have gone astray . . . and the Lord hath laid upon him the iniquity of us all."

Elizabeth later said of this momentous and never-to-be-forgotten time:

> The words were familiar to me; but, as she spoke them, the Holy Spirit's light came into them. I saw all my sins were laid on Jesus; and my whole soul bowed in unutterable worship. . . . [3]
>
> Without a word, without a formal prayer, Jesus stood revealed to me as just, and the justifier of him which believeth. I had what I had longed for—communion with God, in which Jesus would speak to me and I to Him.
>
> And for many nights I could not spare the time for sleep. He made it no difficulty to me to give up all for Him; it came quite natural. Dancing, acting, novels, fashionable dress, jewels, caricaturing, etc., died out of my life by the absorbing power of the new life within. It made me feel I possessed a knowledge which would save men from Hell, and almost all my time was spent in speaking with individuals and seeking to win them to Christ. [4]

She suffered misunderstandings from her family, and former friends passed her on the streets as though she had committed a crime. But she clung to her Savior and witnessed everywhere for and to Him. Her heart, now bound in love to Christ, hungered for more and more of His grace.

God sends both books and people into our lives to help us discover greater heights and depths in the provisions of grace. Both came into Elizabeth's life at this time of trial. Of the book which so greatly helped her she said:

> Some months later, more than half a year after my conversion, although I saw souls continually saved, yet I felt a need for a deeper work of grace. A number of the *Guide to Holiness* was put into my hands, in which was an article by the late Mrs. Phoebe Palmer. I took it to the Lord and, then and there, was led to yield up myself a living sacrifice, and to accept the cleansing from all sin as far as I then understood it, and, in some way, accepted the Holy Ghost to possess me.[5]

An acquaintance with Rev. Aitken of Pendeen, a mighty man of God, proved to be an untold blessing, and Elizabeth wrote of him to this effect:

> He was a very great uplift in my spiritual life. . . . I have in my day heard many blessed preachers of the Gospel, but none with the power from on high which was upon him. His great prayerfulness, his intensity, his knowledge of Scripture, and the presence of God which was always with him, opened indeed a new vista in my spiritual life. There was a greater God-consciousness, a better understanding of the Bible, and a deeper consecration to God and His service.[6]
>
> For eight years after this time, my life seemed to be a going on from strength to strength. It was but a small sphere of labor which God gave me, in a little town and the surrounding villages, but He worked blessedly and gave me, through correspondence and through notes on the Scriptures, an increasing influence.[7]

In 1856, after the family home at Evesham had been broken up, she was asked by Rev. and Mrs. Pennefather to come to Mildmay. As a result of their invitation, she took charge of the deaconesses, devising the well-known Mildmay bonnet and deaconess dress which she herself adopted from that time on. This work at Mildmay led her to the poor of East London, where, during the raging cholera epidemic, she ministered ceaselessly and sacrificially to the sick and the dying.

After two years at Mildmay, circumstances arose which brought about her resignation. As she fervently waited upon God to know the next step of her life, an offer of marriage from Mr. Michael Baxter surprised the thirty-one-year-old deaconess. He had written a book entitled "Louis Napoleon, the Destined Monarch of the World," which created a sensation among Christians. Elizabeth had read it and had corresponded with its author. But it was at a Mildmay Conference where she first met him. He always remembered his first glimpse of her, clad in black, carving at the dinner table with the fair curls hanging about her shoulders.

The marriage was both happy and beneficial to the work of the Lord. We catch a glimpse of Michael Baxter in his biography, written by his son:

> Naturally affectionate, the enthusiastic evangelist longed for a wife sharing his hopes and interests, who would cooperate with him in his mission. For, even in love, his vocation was paramount and, while he craved a helpmeet, he much more desired one who, like himself, put God first, subordinating personal considerations, such as ease or wealth, to the great business of seeking to save the lost.
>
> . . . His choice of a wife was thus decided by his longing for one who felt as he did about the search for the banished and the helpless lost. He was not one to choose lightly, nor apt to be deceived by less than real affection, and he waited until his foreordained bride was brought to him. But he looked out a while for his counterpart. Hence, when he met at Mildmay the lady who was to become his wife, it was with him a case of love, of all his love, at first sight, a grateful surrender of himself to the gift of God.[8]

On their honeymoon, the bride was attracted to the window of their apartment by a familiar voice speaking from outside. The bridegroom was holding an open-air service and announcing a woman speaker for the evening. And so Elizabeth was enlisted early as a partner in his evangelistic efforts.

Elizabeth and Michael were blessed with two children. Rachel, a daughter, brought joy and gladness for only four brief months and then faded away, in spite of all that loving care could do. Michael Paget Baxter, a son who was born the following year, survived his parents, carrying on the work of his father.

After five years of married life, another important development of God's purpose in their lives was made apparent. Mr. Baxter, a great exponent of the second coming of Christ, had been publishing a small monthly magazine entitled, "Signs of Our Times."

When D. L. Moody campaigned in London, the Baxters decided to make the paper a weekly one in which they would keep the public informed of his evangelistic efforts. To the wife, fell the business end of the new venture—reporting, proof-reading, and bookkeeping.

This, along with every-night dealing with anxious souls, resulted in overstrain and a trip to Switzerland was necessitated so that she might regain strength and health. And so a yet wider ministry was opened up for her in Europe. While holding services in Switzerland which proved very effectual, she met Baroness von Gemmingen from Gernsbach, Germany, who invited Elizabeth to visit her.

Although calls from pastors for further evangelism in Switzerland were forthcoming, after a day of fasting and prayer, Mrs. Baxter's impression deepened that God was leading to Germany. The words, "Go to Gernsbach" kept sounding in her soul.

"But, Lord," she inquired, "how about the language? Thou knowest I cannot speak German."

"Never can I forget the answer," she wrote. "It was not in an audible voice, but in the depths of my soul came the answer, 'I can, and I am going with thee.'"

The next morning, she told her husband how her soul had been exercised about the divine call to Germany. "You must do as God tells you," was his reply.

Friends tried to dissuade her from this venture. "But God and my husband being one about it simplified the matter to me," she explained, "and I decided to go to Gernsbach."

Nor did God fail His messenger in the problem of the language barrier, as Mrs. Baxter so remarkably records:

I went downstairs to Frau von Gemmingen and told her that I believed God would have me go to Schauern that evening, and say a few words to the people there. For a long time she used argument after argument to dissuade me from going, and failing, she took me to her husband, who told me that if I went, I should only make a fool of myself, to which I replied that it did not matter to me how foolish I appeared so long as I did the will of God.

He seemed not to understand or believe that God could thus lead me. Then the Baroness said: "There is the deaconess downstairs who teaches the infant school. You shall come to her, and if you can make her understand that you want to have a meeting in her schoolroom, I shall then believe God has sent you." A holy quiet came upon my spirit, and on reaching the room where the deaconess sat, enough German came to my lips to make my request, and she eagerly assented, and said she would gather the women together at the appointed hour.

With a polyglot French and German Bible, God enabled me in the evening to give a little Bible teaching, which I was told, was understood by most. This was indeed truly of the Lord, as the Badische German is a special dialect which I had never before heard spoken; but surely it is as possible to trust the Lord to make people understand what He impels one to speak as it is to trust Him to enable one to teach or preach. He did both that evening, and one soul professed to find peace, and not one only, for her entire family followed her in course of time, turning unto the Lord with full purpose of heart.

Two or three times during the half hour or more that I was speaking, I turned to a friend who was with me to obtain a word, but this hesitation was only for a moment; the speech came, although I was not always acquainted with the full memory of the words which came to me. But the faces of the people showed me that they understood what was being uttered. This was the beginning of blessing, and several more meetings were held, all like the first. The Baron himself attended the second meeting, and was much surprised at what he saw. Yet at table, in the shops, or in any reading other than the Word of God, I could carry on no conversation in German. Oh, pray that my life may be all Gethsemane from henceforth.[9]

But God was fitting His instrument for an even greater field of service. To comfort others and bring healing, she herself must know the depths of pain and suffering. Stricken with a violent form of neuralgia, she spent whole nights in an agony of pain. Letters to her husband at this time reveal the fact that she understood God's purpose in this peculiar trial:

> March 15, 1880: I believe I am near the end of this time of suffering humiliation, for God is making more and more clear where I have been willful in my way of serving Him. He knows I only live to serve Him, but it must be in His way, His time, as well as His strength, bless Him.[10]

> March 23, 1880: God is humbling me as never before. He is so faithful. Oh, that every vestige of self may be done away from me, and then God can have all His will with me. He cannot trust us with power according to the light we have while anything of self remains. I believe I shall praise Him to all eternity for this time of suffering. He would have taught me by other means, but I was not little enough, so He was obliged to use the rod. "Thy rod and thy staff they comfort me."[11]

> April 3, 1880: It gives me a sense of awe to be at ease from pain, as though my life must be more His than ever, and such intense sympathy with those who suffer that I seem to understand Christ. Oh, pray that my life may be all Gethsemane from henceforth.[12]

Those who have had a deeper experience of grace often make the mistake of enshrining it, instead of accepting God's discipline, which is designed to reveal our nothingness and His Almightiness. Mrs. Baxter's writings never could have helped countless perplexed Christians had she not known this divine reduction. In an article written in March, 1887, she said:

> I did not know how much I was occupied at that time with myself and my own holiness. I fell into spiritual pride. This opened the way for other sins of temper, etc. I was sorely disappointed with myself; I felt as though God had failed me. I had conceived a very high and ascetic standard and I had fallen miserably below it, and, though I cried to God for hours by day and hours by night, my old joy and peace did not return.

In the year 1873, I first saw *Gladness in Jesus* by the Rev. W. E. Boardman and, in reading it, my eyes were opened to see that I had been all this time dealing with myself, instead of acting truly to my first consecration of myself to God and letting Him deal with me. All my confidence in my own experience as a savior was gone. My old experience lived again, it is true, but I was on the divine side of it, seeing Jesus as my sanctification, Jesus dwelling in me to be patience in me, love in me, and all else I needed.

From this time, God has been closely educating my conscience. While He keeps me from sinning as I trust Him, He teaches me from time to time His own views of sin, so that things which a year ago were not sin to me, are so now. But the conflict is transferred; the battle is the Lord's. He cleanses; He helps; He fights. I trust and praise Him. He has taught me the same blessed faith for the body as the soul.[13]

An account of Mrs. Baxter's life-message would be incomplete without a few words concerning "Bethshan," a home opened for healing and holiness. This Heaven-blessed establishment was a portion of the fruit of a concern among evangelicals regarding the part that healing plays in the ministry of the Holy Spirit.

Mrs. Baxter earlier had become acquainted with Pastor Stockmayer's ministry at Hauptweil, Samuel Seller's at Mannedorf, and that of others in Europe. As a result, she became exercised about there being a similar testimony in England, showing God's faithfulness to all who trust Him for the needs of body, soul, and spirit.

Meanwhile in America, Dr. Cullis of Boston, grief-stricken at the sudden loss of his young wife, had entered into a deeper union with God. In consequence, he was led to establish a home to prove God's power to cure patients pronounced hopeless by the medical profession.

Rev. W. E. Boardman in England had likewise had a new infusion of grace and he could say: "I seem to float in God and in His will like a bird floats in the air, or a fish in the sea." Often engaged in evangelistic work in America, he visited Dr. Cullis and observed the methods used in his work. Returning to London, he commenced a similar effort in rented premises in the metropolis, which eventually resulted in "Bethshan."

Mrs. Baxter, as God's versatile handmaid, became involved in this ministry, and eventually was the prime mover of this refuge for the sick. She and her husband poured in financial aid, and Bible studies were daily conducted for those desiring to know more of God's purposes in each difficulty. The deeper life of abiding in Jesus was opened to the sufferers, and great was the rejoicing of those who found healing of body as the greater need of the soul was met through the indwelling Comforter. Holiness and healing were dependent upon each other. Writing about the work at "Bethshan," she recounted:

> Many were the healings which took place here, and many were the souls blest. . . . The Rev. Andrew Murray of Wellington, Cape Town, was there as one of our guests. He went into the subject of the Lord's healing very fully and was so convinced that he trusted the Lord himself for healing, helped many, and afterwards wrote a book on the subject.[14]

When several valued associates were called to higher service, Mrs. Baxter realized that this type of ministry had fulfilled its purpose. Its testimony had been borne to the ends of the earth through the pages of the *Christian Herald*, as well as by personal witness.

The perishing multitudes at home and abroad then became her deepest concern, which culminated in the opening of a Training Home where many young people received Christian education before obeying God's call to the mission fields.

Accompanied by Pastor and Mrs. Stockmayer, Mrs. Baxter made a world tour, abundantly fulfilling the promise, "Ye shall be witnesses unto me . . . unto the uttermost part of the earth." Her deep spiritual life also flowed out into forty books on Christian experience, besides numerous booklets and weekly commitments in articles and Bible studies for the *Christian Herald* and other papers.

Mrs. Baxter closed her useful life at the age of eighty-nine years. She had been widowed sixteen years when God took her on December 19, 1926, but her influence lives on in her writings. Before her death, she had voiced the words by which she wished to be remembered, and which were quoted in the special service book prepared for her funeral: "Whenever I may be called away from this world, I should like to have as my testimony, 'God is faithful.'"

QUOTATION BY ELIZABETH BAXTER

God reveals Himself as the great "I Am," and the Lord Jesus, again and again, during the time of His ministry on earth, spake of Himself as "I Am." Now, people almost always tell us what they are and how they feel. Some say, "I am so ignorant!"; some, "I am so sinful"; some, "I am so stupid"; some, "I am so timid." But when the Holy Spirit takes possession of us, He shuts up all the "I am" of our nature, and turns us to the one great "I Am" of God.

It is a glorious life in which God is the "I Am," and in which we take our place by the side of Paul, and say, "I am nothing," or go down even lower to Him Who was "meek and lowly in heart" and say, "I can of mine own self do nothing" (John 5: 30). It is a life in which we expect nothing from ourselves, and in which we know that God expects nothing from us, and if our fellow creatures do, it does not matter to us, because our "life is hid with Christ in God."

The greatest hindrance is your trying to help God to do it, for there is one thing God will never do—He will never mix His work with yours. Yield yourself unreservedly to Him. You say, "I am weak," and you are, but the true "I Am" joins on to that name of His, "the Almighty God."

Where is He almighty? Where He dwells. Just let the Holy Spirit come into you and dwell within you, then His Almightiness walks about with you wherever you go. If Satan tempts you to the old sin, there is almightiness dwelling in Him Who dwells in you, and surely you need not doubt whether the temptation shall be overcome or not. God is equal to it, though you are not.

Shall the "I am" of our self-life be that of Paul: "I am crucified with Christ"? There is an end of me, an end of all my complaining of myself, an end of that old song of what I am—"I am crucified with Christ, nevertheless I live."

Lilias Trotter

THE FRAIL PIONEER

The tall young woman of twenty-three, with light brown hair and a sensitive mouth, roamed the wooded hills that sloped gently down to Coniston Lake, her mind in a turmoil of conflict. Although she had previously visited "Brentwood," the home of John Ruskin, and thoroughly enjoyed the beauty of the surroundings as well as the intellectual and artistic temperament of her host, this time it was different.

John Ruskin had pleaded with Lilias Trotter to reconsider her decision to relinquish the promising pursuit of art, for she had been contemplating the giving of her entire self to another Master in the pursuit of souls. "I pause to think how I can convince you of the marvelous gift that is in you," he had written on a former occasion. Now he was urging her to continue to improve her artistic ability, for he was convinced she would make her mark among foremost artists.

Appreciation of her talent by so famous a man would have been too sore a temptation had not the "love of One that is stronger" reached out and touched her heart. The die was cast. Turning her back upon a future so bright with promise, she summed up her decision thus: "I see as clear as daylight now I cannot give myself to painting in the way he (John Ruskin) means and continue still 'to seek . . . first the kingdom of God and his righteousness.'"

Everything in the life of Lilias Trotter had favored her career as an artist. Nature had richly endowed her. The circumstances into which she was born, in 1853, provided financial security while she studied. Her father, of Scottish parentage, was "a charming character of love, generosity, and gentleness, combined with high qualities of intellect and acquirements." He always had encouraged his nine children in their pursuit of scientific and artistic studies. He had procured French and German governesses for them, and frequent visits to the Continent had given them that poise which only widely traveled persons acquire.

Her mother was Isabella Strange, whose father had been Chief Justice of Halifax, Nova Scotia. Although she was the second wife of Alexander Trotter, she proved a good and able mother to his six children by his former wife. Three more children by the second marriage were added to their spacious home. Lilias was the first of these three.

The girl, sensitive to a degree, keenly felt the blow that fell upon the family, when her beloved father was taken from them when she was only twelve. But her grief created in her a response to the love of her Savior. When others thought her away playing with her dolls, she was spending the time in prayer.

When Lilias was twenty-one years of age, she and her mother attended a convention at "Broadlands," convened by Lord Mount-Temple, a Christian statesman. The speakers that year were Andrew Jukes, Theodore Monod, and the American Quakeress, Mrs. Pearsall Smith, author of *The Christian's Secret of a Happy Life*. The messages given were on the theme of consecration and God's gift of His Holy Spirit. Her eyes "were opened to see the loveliness of the Son of God and His right to control her redeemed life."

The next year, another event helped to shape the character of this impressionable young woman. D. L. Moody came to London and she and one of her sisters attended these services and sang in the choir. Lilias was profoundly impressed with the evangelistic fervor exhibited night after night which resulted in the salvation of souls.

The Y.W.C.A. was achieving success among working girls, and Lilias and a friend rented a music hall, turning it into a hostel for these young women. Prayer-meetings were frequently called during the conducting of special services, and sometimes all nights of prayer were engaged in that the forces of evil might be defeated in many lives. As a result, contacts were made with girls whose "business" was sin and with some of whom Lilias prayed into the early hours of the morning.

In 1876, Mrs. Trotter and her daughter traveled to Venice. A letter of Ruskin's tells how he discovered the latent talent in this budding artist:

When I was at Venice in 1876—it is about the only thing that makes me now content in having gone there—two English ladies, mother and daughter, were staying at the same hotel, the "Europa." One day the mother sent me a pretty little note asking if I would look at the young lady's drawings.

On my somewhat sulky permission, a few were sent, in which I saw there was extremely right-minded and careful work, almost totally without knowledge. I sent back a request that the young lady might be allowed to come out sketching with me. She seemed to learn everything the instant she was shown it, and ever so much more than she was taught.[1]

Ruskin displayed her drawings and from that time became her friend and champion. Not understanding the love that had drawn this young woman to spend her life in work for women of the street he wrote:

Am I not bad enough?
Am I not good enough?
Am I not whatever it is enough, to be looked after a little when I am ill, as well as those blessed Magdalenes?[2]

But her work among the girls she loved continued to absorb Lilias' time and strength for the next ten years. And the reason for such devotion and sacrifice is expressed in one of her favorite hymns:

A homeless Stranger amongst us came
        To this land of death and mourning,
He walked in a path of sorrow and shame,
        Through insult and hate and scorning.

A Man of sorrows, of toil and tears,
        An outcast Man and a lonely,
But He looked on me and through endless years
        Him must I love, Him only.

Then from this sad and sorrowful land,
        From this land of tears, He departed;
But the light of His eyes, and the touch of His hand,
        Had left me brokenhearted.[3]

During this same period, she made the acquaintance of two women whose influence was to change the direction of her labors for more than forty years. Lilias wrote later:

> I quite expected to spend my life in the Y.W.C.A. and was not interested in missionary work, but I was thrown a good deal with Adeline Braithwaite and Lelie Duff, and I felt that both of them had taken to heart the outer darkness in a way I had not. I do not remember that they said anything to me personally about it, but one felt it right through them. They were all aglow. I saw that they had a fellowship with Jesus that I knew nothing about. So I began to pray, "Lord, give me the fellowship with Thee over the heathen that Thou hast given to these two!"
>
> It was not many weeks before it began to come—a strange, yearning love over those who were "in the land of the shadow of death"—a feeling that Jesus could speak to me about them, and that I could speak to Him—that a great barrier between Him and me had been broken right down and swept away.
>
> I had no thought of leaving England then, no thought even at first of trying to stir others at home. But, straight as a line, God made my way out into the darkness before eighteen months were over. And through eternity I shall thank Him for the silent flame in the hearts of those two friends, and what it did for me. Neither of them has ever had her path opened into foreign work, but the light of the Day that is coming will show what He has let them do in kindling other souls."[4]

Whenever Lilias prayed, the words, "North Africa," sounded in her soul as though a voice were calling her. In May, 1887, a missionary meeting was held by Mr. Glenny who spoke on the needs of that field. When the appeal was made at the end of the service, Lilias arose and said, "God is calling me." In less than a year, she had reached Africa, accompanied by two other young women. Her favorite song once more became her own testimony:

> And I clave to Him as He turned His face
> From the land that was mine no longer;
> The land I had loved in the ancient days,
> Ere I knew the love that was stronger.

> And I would abide where He abode,
> And follow His steps for ever;
> His people my people, His God my God,
> In the land beyond the river.

In a letter home, she wrote:

> I would not be anywhere else but in this hardest of fields with an invincible Christ. None of us would have been passed by a doctor for any missionary society. We did not know a soul in the place, or a sentence of Arabic, nor had we a clue as to how to begin work on such untouched ground. We only knew we had to come. If God needed weakness, He had it! We were on a fool's errand, so it seemed, and we are on it still, and glory in it. For the Moslem world that has challenged Christ for over twelve centuries has not had His last word yet.[5]

The intrepid young missionaries rented a big, fortress-like house in Algiers. Rumor had it that it was three hundred years old. Their front door was known for a long time as "the door of a thousand dents," as unruly boys and opposing adults battered at its rugged thickness. Those were most difficult years for these pioneers for they faced hostility, suspicion by authorities, and the inborn hatred of Islam for Christ.

After seven years on the Moslem field, Lilias returned to England with badly frayed nerves and heart worn by strain and stress. The extreme heat, too, had been most debilitating. How she appreciated the quietness and aloneness of the homeland, where she could regain the apparently lost powers of body, soul, and spirit!

As the quiet entered into her very soul, God began to make further revelations to her of what it meant to be "buried" with Christ! She writes:

> Not only "dead" but "buried," put to silence in the grave; the "I can't," and the "I can," put to silence side by side in the stillness of "a grave beside Him" with God's seal on the stone and His watch set that nothing but the risen life of Jesus may come forth.

"Give me a death in which there shall be no life, and a life in which there shall be no death." That was the prayer of an Arab saint, Abed-al-Kadar. I came upon it the other day. Is it not wonderful![6]

It was now that she saw the loathsomeness of all that is of the flesh and not of the Spirit. The lesson had been taught by the messengers of disappointments, seeming failure, and frustrations. Two of the most promising women converts died as a result of slow poisoning. Another had fallen under the spell of a sorceress. Five out of six backslidings, the missionaries concluded, could be traced to the drugging of the converts. Lilias and her friends would have welcomed the triumphant entry into Heaven of any newly converted, rather than to have seen their minds and bodies despoiled under drug reaction. They were driven to the throne of grace for, without divine aid, helpless women in a hostile Moslem land could not possibly counter such satanic forces.

She might well have been thinking of this period of opposition, when she wrote:

> I am full of hope that when God delays in fulfilling our little thoughts, it is to leave Himself room to work out His great ones. And, more and more as time goes on, I feel that the longer He waits the more we can expect, for the deeper and wider will be the undermining, and the greater will be the band of those who will come forth free from their prison walls. When one gets hold of that vision, one can throw back in the devil's face his taunts over the seemingly wasted years that lie behind us.

One day, a most unusual opportunity arose to introduce the work of the Algier's Mission Band to six hundred American delegates from the World's Sunday School Convention who were en route to Rome. Scheduled to land for a short time in Algiers, they asked for one hour with Miss Trotter that they might become acquainted with the Christian effort among the Moslems.

With no hospitals, no schools, little organization, and few apparent results to show for the twenty years' labor, dismay filled her heart at the request. How could she hope to make these keen and successful business men understand? The missionaries brought the problem to God, believing that "difficulty is the very atmosphere of miracle." They decided to show, not what had been done, but what had not been done, trusting Him to use the very weakness and seeming failure to interest the group. And God did just that, for the American delegates became fast friends of the Mission in Algeria for years to come. During the twenty years, in reality, much had been accomplished. Centers had been opened in strategic places; travel by train and camel had taken the missionaries to remote and almost inaccessible parts where they could broadcast the message of redeeming love.

But times of illness came to Lilias. These hours, however, were not spent in an idle fashion but rather devoted to writing. She penned *Parables of the Cross*, in which she also utilized her artistic ability by drawing lovely illustrations from nature for its pages. She aided friends in a revision of the Bible in classical Arabic. As a result of this effort, the Gospels of Luke and John were widely distributed in the area.

Feeling the need for Moslem mystics, she wrote *The Way of the Sevenfold Secret* on the seven "I Am's." She was sure if Christian literature could but find its way into the homes of the Arabic world, it would be read without the opposition encountered in public effort. Probably Lilias did more in her preparation of reading material for the people than in her personal contacts, for her knowledge of the country, familiarity with the language, and experience with the opposition—all this made the literature much more effective in its presentation of the Gospel.

The last three years of Lilias' life were marked by extremely limited strength. Her heart, so worn from the soldiering, probably would not have functioned at all save for the warrior spirit within. From her bed, propped up by pillows, she directed the work of the Band, praying for each worker by name during the night watches when sleep refused to come.

To the very end, the worker was being molded by the Master into greater conformity to His image. While the citadel of her heart had long since been captured, there were areas of the natural life, such as her sympathetic disposition which needed to be brought into subjection to the Master. In her own words:

It has opened out to one a whole new era that has to be subdued unto Himself—the region of natural temperament that lies at
the back of the self-life in man, which needs to be transformed by
the renewing of our minds. Transformed does not mean annihi-
lated, but transfigured by a new indwelling. He can take that very
susceptibleness that has been a snare and make it a means of contact with Himself, a sensitiveness to the Holy Ghost. It is worth all
the humbling and heart-searching and the breaking up of depths
after depths, if it means getting nearer the place where the living
water will be set free.[7]

In another quotation from her pen, she portrays the growing
sway of the Spirit's dominion in her:

In a stream which is ankle deep, one can walk where one will.
When it is knee-deep, the "pull" has begun. When it is to the loins,
"the drawing" has become almost irresistible. And the next thing is
that it cannot "be passed over"; they are "waters to swim in." "Borne
on unto perfection" is the literal meaning in Hebrews 6:1. "There
the glorious Lord will be unto us a place of broad rivers and streams"
(Isa. 33:21).[8]

This saint who had chosen to share the life of her risen Lord
rather than to enjoy the honors a fickle world could heap upon her,
had partaken deeply of that divine Partner's secrets. In a booklet, *A
Ripened Life*, she shares with us the deep insights she had obtained
through close communion:

"In that day there shall be upon the bridles of the horses. Holiness Unto the Lord." The horse seems to stand throughout the
Old Testament for natural power. In each of us there is one strongest point; it may be brain power, or some faculty, as music for
instance, or the power of planning, the power of influence, the
power of loving. And, whatever it may be, that strong point is sure
to be a point of temptation, just as their horses were a temptation
to Israel.

Trace the history. In spite of God's warning (Deut. 17:16)
they "multiplied" them (1 Kings 4:26; 10:28) and "trusted in them"
(Isa. 31:1), and by this multiplying, power was put into the hands of

their enemies (1 Kings 10:29) which was afterwards turned round upon themselves for their own ruin.

Can we not, some of us, read our own story between the lines? Have we not given play to these faculties, "multiplied" them so to speak, for the sake of the exultant sense of growing power, not for God? Have we not trusted in our horses? In the well-worked-out "subject" for instance, rather than in the Spirit's might? Have we not been brought into soul-captivity by means of self indulgence in these faculties, God-created though they are? And therefore most of us, as we go on, find that God's hand comes down on the strongest parts of us, as it came upon the horses of Israel (Zech. 12:4; Hos. 1:7). By outward providence or by inward dealing, He brings it to the place of death, and to the place where we lose our hold on it and our trust in it and say with Ephraim, "We will not ride upon horses" (Hos. 14:3). And in that place of death, God may leave it for months and years till the old glow of life has really died out of it, and the old magical charm has vanished, and it has become no effort to do without it because life's current has gone into the current of God's will.

Then comes the day as in Israel's case before us, when He can give us back our horses with "Holiness to the Lord" written on them, bridled with Christ-restraint. Where are our horses? Are we riding them in their old natural force, or are they lying stiffened and useless in the place of death, or have they been given back to us with their holy bridles?

Weeks of suffering began in May, 1928, but Lilias' mind retained its clearness, and she never lost sight of the "Master of the Impossible." As the end drew near, looking out of her window, she exclaimed, "A chariot and six horses!"

"You are seeing beautiful things," said a friend.

"Yes, many, many beautiful things," was the joyful and last response to those around her. Had the chariot borne her to Heaven, as it had the prophet Elijah? We do not know. But we can be assured that the trumpets of the angels sounded for the arrival of the Christian warrior who had dared, at the call of "the invincible Christ," to leave earthly comfort, ease, fame, and friends, for an unknown land.

And where He died would I also die:
For dearer a grave beside Him,
Than a kingly place among living men,
The place which they denied Him.

QUOTATIONS BY LILIAS TROTTER

Oh, for an enthusiasm for Christ that will not endure to be popular where He is unpopular; that will be fired rather than quenched when His claims are unrecognized and His Word is slighted; that will thrill us with joy if He allows us to share in the faintest degree in His dishonor and loneliness; that will set every pulse throbbing with exultation as we "go forth . . . unto him."

Emptiness, yieldedness, brokenness—these are the conditions of the Spirit's outflow. Such was the path taken by the Prince of Life to set free the flood-tide of Pentecost.

Oh, the pains that God has to take to bring us to this "abandon"—equally ready for silence or for saying, for stillness or for doing unhesitatingly the next thing He calls for, unfettered by surroundings or consequences. How much reserve and self-consciousness have to give way with some of us before the absolute control passes into His hands and the responsibility with it.

John Hyde
THE PRAYING MISSIONARY

The congregation waited expectantly for the speaker, who had for two nights previously given messages rich in content, to begin his message. But John Hyde, though fully prepared, remained silent. "For two days," said one present at that conference, "he came before the convention, stating that he was not allowed to give further addresses until the challenge of the first address was accepted and the Holy Spirit given rightful place. He called all to prayer and then remained silent. He at first sustained violent criticism, but his critics were broken under the power of the Spirit, and Hyde's obedience meant for the Punjab Church many a Spirit-filled worker."[1]

A backward look at the life and discipline of this man of prayer enables us to understand how he became a vessel that God could use.

John Hyde was the son of a minister. From the year of his birth in 1865 until 1882, the family lived in Carrolton, Illinois, U.S.A. The home of Dr. Smith Hyde was one of culture and refinement to which was added the influence of religion in its reality. The fervency of his parents at the family altar greatly contributed to John's ultimate power in intercessory prayer.

When his father accepted the pastorate of a Presbyterian Church in Carthage, Illinois, John enrolled as a student in that town. His scholastic ability was so outstanding that after graduation he was asked to become a teacher in his alma mater. That profession had no attraction for the young man and, in obedience to what he felt was the call of God, he decided to attend a seminary in the city of Chicago.

At a missionary meeting where the need of workers for foreign service was powerfully presented, John's soul was stirred. Later, he sought out a fellow-student who had assisted in the program, demanding, "Give me all the arguments you have for the foreign field."

"You do not need arguments," retorted his friend. "What you want to do is to get down on your knees and stay there until the matter is settled one way or another."

And Hyde did just that. As he waited upon God, he was convinced that the divine plan for him could be fulfilled only somewhere beyond the sea. From that time, foreign service was his chief topic of conversation. His prayers were to the end that his classmates, too, should see the fields white to harvest in lands where Christ was not known. His fervent petitions were abundantly answered for, from his class of forty-six graduates, twenty-six offered themselves for foreign missionary effort.

John set sail for India after graduation in October, 1892, with mixed ambitions. To be sure, he wished to rescue the perishing among India's millions, but he also hoped to make a name for himself, to so master the languages necessary that eventually he would become a missionary of fame. When he went to his cabin, he found a letter addressed to him in a familiar handwriting. It was that of a ministerial friend of his father, one whom the young man greatly admired for the depth of his spiritual life. As he read, he was startled. "I shall not cease praying for you, dear John, until you are filled with the Holy Spirit." Clearly the implication was that he was not so filled. He confessed later:

> My pride was touched, and I felt exceedingly angry, crushed the letter, threw it into a corner of the cabin, and went up on deck. I loved the writer; I knew the holy life he lived. And down in my heart was the conviction that he was right, and I was not fitted to be a missionary. . . .
>
> In despair, I asked the Lord to fill me with the Holy Spirit, and the moment I did this the whole atmosphere was cleared up. I began to see myself and what a selfish ambition I had. It was a struggle almost to the end of the voyage, but I was determined long before the port was reached that, whatever the cost, I would be really filled with the Spirit."[2]

When he arrived in India, John attended a meeting where, in no uncertain way, the fact was emphasized that Jesus Christ is able to save from all sin. When one of the listeners, at the close of the service, approached the speaker with the pointed question, "Is that your personal experience?" John was extremely thankful that he had not been thus questioned. He acknowledged to himself that, although he had been preaching such a Gospel, experimentally he was a stranger to its power.

Plainly there was no side-stepping the spiritual issue now confronting him. Without the baptism with the Holy Spirit experienced by the 120 at Pentecost in the upper room in Jerusalem, he was a complete failure. He retired to his room, saying to God, "Either Thou must give me victory over all my sin, and especially over the sin that so easily besets me, or I shall return to America to seek there for some other work. I am unable to preach the Gospel until I can testify to its power in my own life."[3]

John was now where God wanted him. In simple faith, he looked to Christ for the deliverance from sin for which his heart was craving. He said later, "He did deliver me, and I have not had a doubt of this since. I can now stand up without hesitation to testify that He has given me victory."

He found the language somewhat difficult for several reasons. One was that he was slightly deaf. Another was the fact that he believed a thorough knowledge of God's Word to be more important to his success as a missionary than anything else. When the examining committee showed dissatisfaction at John's lack of progress in the vernacular of the people among whom he had come to labor, his answer was, "I must put first things first." In time, however, he did acquire such a command of several languages of India that he spoke with almost native fluency.

God wisely trains the instrument which He intends greatly to use by bringing most unexpected and often most undesirable providences into his life. In 1898, John was laid aside for seven months. He took typhoid fever which was followed by two abscesses in his back. This produced a nervous depression which necessitated absolute rest. Writing of this period, he says:

> For a long time after my illness of last May, nervous weakness kept me in the hills, though I wished much to go back to work. . . . All during the year, the prayer of Jabez recorded in 1 Chron. 4:10 kept flooding the soul with its melody. "Enlarge my borders," it sang, day by day, for weeks on end. . . . The answer was an illness, straitening and limiting strength and efforts—taking me, keeping

me from working for months, pressing home lessons of waiting, impressing the great lesson, "Not my will, but Thine, be done." But with the waiting and straitening came spiritual enlarging. How often God withholds the temporal, or delays it, that we may long for and seek the spiritual.[4]

For twenty years, with an interlude of one furlough because of ill health, Hyde labored in the villages of India. With a tent and a few native workers, he traveled from place to place, proclaiming the good news of salvation. He prayed constantly for a work of the Holy Spirit among India's darkened populace. He believed his petitions would be answered for, said he, "If the heart be right, blessing cannot be withheld; it can only be delayed."

At the beginning of 1899, out of the depths of disappointment over few conversions among the heathen, he was led into a depth of prayer life not hitherto realized. With the world excluded, he often wrestled with God until midnight. Or, before the rising sun of a new day, he was on his knees, pleading for an outpouring of divine grace upon the villages of India.

In 1902, John returned to America to regain health. There he emphasized again and again the necessity of the Spirit's infilling in hearts everywhere, if the cause of missions was to advance. Citing Pentecost as proof, he declared that united prayer on the part of Christians would produce a tremendous enlargement of the Church at home and abroad.

On his return to India, revival came to the school for girls at Sialkot, in the Punjab, the headquarters of the United Presbyterian Mission under which John labored. It was marked by open and public confession of sin and clear-cut conversions.

The Spirit of God also moved upon the nearby seminary. Some of the theological students, aflame with divine love, visited the school for boys where, strange to tell, they were not permitted to witness to what God had done for them. The young men returned to the seminary, where they and others united in prayer for a visitation of the Holy Spirit upon that branch of the work. "Oh, Lord," they pleaded, "please grant that the place where we were forbidden to speak tonight may become the center from which great blessings shall flow to all parts of India."

The management of the boys' school soon was placed in other hands, and a convention at Sialkot was announced in April, 1904. The purpose was to unite in prayer for a movement of the Spirit of God throughout India. Only a few truly praying Christians responded to the invitation, among them, John Hyde. Another prayer session was decided upon in August. As a prelude, John and a friend spent thirty days and nights in earnest supplication for a revival.

Canon Haslam was present at that gathering and, twenty-eight years later, in a lecture on Hyde, gave his personal impression of the services and of the remarkable change which took place in him.

> Shortly after the commencement of convention proper, Mr. Hyde passed through an experience that made him what he became—a man who had power with God and a truly great missionary. I have always thought of this change as vicarious repentance and confession in behalf of the whole Church. . . .
>
> During the growth of the Church, many from the outcast population had been baptized and, doubtless, were Christians, but the life of the Church as a whole, was at a low ebb spiritually. Something drastic was needed. . . . To Hyde it was revealed that the Church had no power because of sin which had not been cleansed from her life, and that sin is washed away only when there is true repentance and confession.
>
> He was a part of that Church. Burdened with this thought, after an all-night vigil and a day of fasting and prayer, he came into the presence of a large group of Indian Christian men and spoke openly, though reservedly and in much anguish of spirit, of his personal conflict with secret sin that was ofttimes repeated, and of how God had led him through to victory. The effect of this open confession was electric. . . . That experience marked the beginning of a life of great spiritual power in the case of John Hyde and the beginning of a deep revival in the Punjab Church.[5]

John himself caught a fresh vision of the doctrine of holiness. His Bible readings were marked, not only by a deeper personal understanding of divine truths, but also by the ability to convey them to others.

The Sialkot Convention of 1905 was preceded by much prayer. The glorious result was that, at the close of the first service, the entire congregation went to their knees, continuing in prayer and confession of spiritual deflection until the dawn of day. From that time, the United Presbyterian Mission at Sialkot was lifted onto a higher spiritual plane than it had ever been reached previously. "Good" missionaries became known as "powerful" ones. The effect was felt throughout all India, and the breath of Heaven sweeping over the land could be traced to the kneeling figure of "praying" Hyde.

Only seven more years of labor remained for God's servant. During that time, John entered deeply into the spirit of intercession. Prayer literally became his meat and drink, so much so that the physical side of his nature seemed to be lifted above its normal needs.

Some time during 1908, he began to pray for the conversion of one soul a day. In village treks or in tent services, he lost no opportunity to press the claims of God upon many or few. At the end of the year, to his knowledge, there had been four hundred conversions and baptisms. To God he gave the glory, but the goal set for the next twelve months was two conversions daily. Again Hyde's faith and intercessory prayers were rewarded and, at the year's end, through his contacts, eight hundred persons were known to have come to the Savior.

The last convention he attended was in 1910, for his health was failing. Pleading with God for the conversion of four souls each day, divine assurance was given him that such would be the case. Often more than that number would be given in answer to his prayers, and this lifted Hyde's heart to God in songs of praise and thanksgiving. "There was nothing superficial about the life of those converts. They nearly all became active Christians," was the comment of one who was on the field and thus able to appraise the results.

"Praying" Hyde had learned a most valuable secret of maintaining the spiritual life. One of his closest fellow-laborers, Pengwern Jones, remembered a convention sermon given by John which left its impress upon his life. He said:

I think that the Spirit used him to give us all an entirely new vision of the Cross. That was one of the most inspiring messages I ever heard. He began the address by saying that from whatever side or direction we look at Christ on the cross, we see wounds, we see signs of suffering. From above, we see the marks of the crown of thorns; from behind the cross, we see the furrows caused by the scourging, etc. He dwelt on the Cross with such illumination that we forgot Hyde and everyone else. The "dying, yet living Christ" was before us. Then, step by step, we were led to see the crucified Christ a sufficiency for every need of ours and, as he dwelt on the fitness of Christ for every emergency, I felt that I had sufficient for time and eternity.

But the climax of all to me was the way he emphasized the truth that Christ on the cross cried out triumphantly, "It is finished," when all around thought that His life had ended. It seemed to His disciples that He had failed to carry out His purposes; it appeared to His enemies that at last their dangerous "enemy" had been overcome. To all appearances, the struggle was over, and His life had come to a tragic end. Then the triumphant cry of victory was sounded out, "It is finished." A cry of triumph in the darkest hour!

Then Hyde showed us that, if united to Christ, we can also shout triumphantly, even when everything points to despair. Though our work may appear to have failed and the enemy to have gained the ascendancy, and we are blamed by all our friends and pitied by all our fellow-workers, even then we can take our stand with Christ on the cross and shout out, "Victory, victory, victory!"

From that day, I have never been in despair about my work. Whenever I feel despondent, I think I hear Hyde's voice shouting, "Victory!" And that immediately takes my thoughts to Calvary, and I hear my Savior in His dying hour crying out with joy, "It is finished." As Hyde said, "This is real victory, to shout triumphantly though all around is darkness."

Another close friend, R. McChyene Paterson, discloses what he feels to be the secret of John's extraordinary success:

This dependence upon Christ and His Spirit was the secret of John Hyde's success in everything. This is the open secret of every saint of God! "My strength blossoms out to perfection in weakness," is His Word. So "when I am weak, I am strong"—strong

with divine strength. The more we grow in grace, the more dependent we become! Never let us forget this glorious fact, and then we
shall be able to thank God for our bad memories, for our weak
bodies, for everything, and in that sacrifice of praise shall be His
delight and also our own. So this fruit shall fill the whole earth!

The sands of time were running out for this man of God, and a
serious heart condition developed, one that required an undetermined
period of rest. Early in 1911, John sailed for America, where it was
learned he was suffering also from a brain tumor. An operation
brought only temporary relief and, in less than a year after leaving
his beloved India, John Hyde said farewell to this world, with the
words in Hindi upon his lips, "Shout the victory of Jesus Christ."[6]

Certain it is that high on the honor roll of God, both in earth
and in Heaven, is inscribed ineffaceably the name of Praying Hyde,
intercessor for the lost.

A LITTLE FARTHER

A little farther, let me go with Thee
To share the travail of Gethsemane;
O let me watch with Thee for this last hour,
And for the conflict prove Thy Spirit's power.

A little farther still, I go with Thee,
Right up the hill to lonely Calvary,
To death of all that robs my life of Thee,
That Thou may'st pour afresh Thy life through me.

A little farther yet until I see
Thy straying sheep who wander far from Thee;
Then love divine shall cause my heart to glow,
And all ablaze for God I forth shall go.

A little farther, seeing just ahead
The very footprints of my Master's tread;
A little farther still, and I shall be
Safe in the Gloryland at Home with Thee.

—*Mary Bazeley.*

Samuel Logan Brengle

SOLDIER AND SERVANT

Who would have thought it! Young, formerly ambitious Brengle on his knees polishing eighteen pair of boots! He who had turned down the call to a popular pulpit of a large Methodist Church in an American city was actually performing this most menial task in the Salvation Army Training Barracks in London. The struggle was sharp but short. He wondered if all his educational advantages and personal talents were being thrown away. Then the Holy Spirit brought to his remembrance his Great Exemplar. "If Jesus could wash the disciples' feet, I can blacken the Cadets' boots!" was the happy conclusion. And so young Brengle accepted cheerfully William Booth's rigorous methods of training soldiers of the Cross, and for almost half a century he was to be a highly used specialist in promoting a deep concept of consecration and holy living in the worldwide circle of Salvation Army influence.

Samuel Logan Brengle was born in Fredericksburg, Indiana, U.S.A., of William and Rebecca Brengle, June 1, 1860. When the lad was two years of age, his schoolteacher father responded to the call of his country to serve in the Northern Army during the American Civil War. Wounded in the siege of Vicksburg, the brave young soldier returned home only to succumb to his wounds. The godly wife and mother, now entrusted with the rearing of her only child, faithfully instructed him in the things of God. Although she married again and life consisted of one move after another, attendance at church never was neglected.

Revival services came to the small town of Olney, Illinois, where the family lived, and the young Samuel sought for peace of heart at the close of each service. For five nights in succession, he knelt in prayer, believing that such an act of decision would make him a Christian. But no divine witness followed.

Some time later, in a walk with his mother, they talked together concerning the latest proposed move to Texas of the ever restless stepfather. "Mother," exclaimed Samuel, "I'm glad we didn't move to Texas. If we had, I might have fallen in with a rough, drunken lot of fellows and lost my soul. But we stayed here, and I have become a Christian." With this declaration, there came such a sense of peace and rest of soul that he knew beyond all doubt he was accepted of God. For weeks, he reveled in his Heaven-sent experience. But the work of redemption within was not complete as he was yet to learn.

As he walked home from school one day with several companions, an argument arose, whereupon one of the boys called Sam a most undesirable name. Then and there, young Brengle became aware of the presence of evil within his heart as, in retaliation, he dealt a hearty blow with the fist. Immediately the wonted calm of his soul was exchanged for a storm of confusion and distress. Nor could he feel a sense of rightness with his Maker until he had sought forgiveness at the throne of grace for the unseemly act.

Throwing himself heartily into church work at fifteen years of age, he became assistant superintendent of the Sunday School. His eagerness for knowledge led his high school teachers to recommend that he study grammar with an excellent professor who lived about fifteen miles distant. His mother consented to this agreement, though the close relationship existing between her and Samuel made the parting mutually painful.

The lad was thrown into a most bewildering emotional state when his mother, after a brief illness, passed away. His sorrow seemed to be assuaged only by a closer application to his studies and, as he advanced in them, the next step in his career was college. The sale of the farm provided funds. And Brengle, at seventeen years of age, enrolled as a student in what is now DePauw University in Greencastle, Indiana.

His college career marked him as a brilliant scholar, particularly in oratory, and ambitions of a political nature began to appear on the horizon of his life. But God had another plan for Brengle, which now and again flitted across his vision although he was almost unwilling to acknowledge its existence—a plan that he should become a preacher of the Gospel. In a somewhat unusual way, he was led to comply.

Because of his natural eloquence, he was chosen to speak at an annual convention upon an important matter on which depended the very life of the fraternity to which he belonged. He was so burdened with the sense of responsibility entailed, that in anguish of spirit he prayed for divine help, vowing that if his speech accomplished its purpose he would yield the point and obey God wherever His call led him. When his prayer was answered, he could not disregard the blueprint for his life that God had at various times tried to reveal to him.

After graduation, Samuel served for a brief time as a circuit preacher of the Methodist Church. Then friends advised him to take up the study of theology and, spurred by the ambition to become a preacher of note, Brengle enrolled at Boston Theological Seminary.

This decision ushered in the most important experience of his career. For eight years, he had been painfully aware of an inner conflict between the forces of good and of evil within his own heart, with no clear knowledge as to the way the problem could be solved. In Boston he was blessed, just when he needed it most, by the instruction of Dr. Daniel Steele concerning the provision of Calvary for the sin of his wayward heart. This godly tutor was able to prove from the Scripture that inner deliverance was possible, and he could also confirm the reality by personal testimony. How timely was this Heaven-planned contact! And much study brought to his aid a greater Teacher than Steele—the Holy Spirit Himself. He describes what this Teacher revealed to his hungry heart:

> I saw the humility of Jesus and my pride; the meekness of Jesus and my temper; the lowliness of Jesus and my ambition; the purity of Jesus and my unclean heart; the faithfulness of Jesus and the deceitfulness of my heart; the unselfishness of Jesus and my selfishness; the trust and faith of Jesus and my doubts and unbelief; the holiness of Jesus and my unholiness. I got my eyes off everybody but Jesus and myself, and I came to loathe myself.[1]

Interwoven with the knowledge that God had called him to preach, was the ignoble yet insistent urge to be a big preacher. How subtle was the temptation, "If I can only be a great preacher like Moody! Perhaps if I seek the baptism, I shall have this power!" And he further adds, "I was seeking the Holy Spirit that I might use Him, rather than that He might use me."

The morning of January 9, 1895, found Brengle awake early, his soul stirred to the depths. The Spirit of God was trying to bring him to a definite issue. "Today," exclaimed the young man, "I must obtain—or be lost forever." But his ambition for ministerial greatness had not yet been brought to the Cross, although he prayed, "Lord, if Thou wilt only sanctify me, I will take the meanest little appointment there is."

His carnal heart, meanwhile, found comfort in the thought that even though he should be assigned to a small, obscure church, he could still be a powerful speaker. Then a flash of divine light discovered the enormity of his love of self to such an extent that, broken completely before the revelation, he exclaimed, "Lord, I wanted to be an eloquent preacher but, if by stammering and stuttering, I can bring greater glory to Thee than by eloquence, then let me stammer and stutter." But the Holy Spirit delayed His coming. Suddenly, however, the darkness of his soul was pierced by the words, "If we confess our sins, he is faithful and just to forgive us our sins, and to cleanse us from all unrighteousness."

"I believe that," was Brengle's response, and then the Lord Whom he sought came suddenly to His temple. To the end of his days, Brengle never doubted the reality of this work of grace in his soul, nor did he ever cease to magnify it. Two days later, another manifestation of God flooded his soul. Of this experience, he said:

> I opened my Bible and, while reading some of the words of Jesus, He gave me such a blessing as I never had dreamed a man could have this side of Heaven. It was an unutterable revelation. It was a Heaven of love that came into my heart. My soul melted like wax before fire. I sobbed and sobbed. I loathed myself that I had ever sinned against Him or doubted Him or lived for myself and not for His glory. Every ambition for self was now gone. The pure flame of love burned like a blazing fire would burn a moth.

I walked out over Boston Commons before breakfast, weeping for joy and praising God. Oh, how I loved! In that hour I knew Jesus, and I loved Him till it seemed my heart would break with love. I was filled with love for all His creatures. I heard the little sparrows chattering; I loved them. I saw a little worm wriggling across my path; I stepped over it; I didn't want to hurt any living thing. I loved the dogs; I loved the horses; I loved the little urchins on the street; I loved the strangers who hurried past me; I loved the heathen; I loved the whole world.[2]

To be sure, such a flood-tide of emotion subsided, but in its place came the certainty and solidity of an unwavering faith that made Brengle the spiritual giant he became. Again he writes:

One day, with amazement, I said to a friend, "This is the perfect love about which the apostle John wrote, but it is beyond all I dreamed of; in it is personality. This love thinks, wills, talks with me, corrects me, instructs me, and teaches me." And then I knew that God, the Holy Ghost, was in this love, and that this love was God, for "God is love."

Oh, the rapture mingled with reverential, holy fear—for it is a rapturous, yet divinely fearful thing—to be indwelt by the Holy Ghost, to be a temple of the living God! Great heights are always opposite great depths, and, from the heights of this blessed experience, many have plunged into the dark depths of fanaticism. But we must not draw back from the experience through fear. All danger will be avoided by meekness and lowliness of heart, by humble, faithful service, by esteeming others better than ourselves, and in honor preferring them before ourselves, by keeping an open, teachable spirit, in a word, by looking steadily unto Jesus, to Whom the Holy Spirit continually points us; for He would not have us fix our attention exclusively upon Himself and His work in us, but also upon the Crucified One and His work for us, that we may walk in the steps of Him Whose blood purchases our pardon and makes and keeps us clean.

Doors of opportunity swung open. The flattering offer of the pastorate of the largest Methodist church in the northern part of the state of Indiana formerly would have been accepted without hesitation. Now it was rejected. Brengle felt that divine guidance was directing him to the Salvation Army. He had heard General Booth speak and had been greatly moved. The open-air efforts of those intrepid warriors of the Cross had a strange appeal and, when a Voice whispered, "These are My people," the die was cast. He determined to go to England, where he could personally offer himself to General Booth and where he could receive adequate training for Christian service.

He had become engaged to a young Salvationist, Elizabeth Swift. In every way, she seemed to meet the high standards he had set for himself concerning marriage and, with her full consent, he set sail for England two days after the wedding.

General Booth eyed Brengle coolly. "You belong to the dangerous classes," he said. "You have been your own boss for so long that I don't think you will want to submit to Salvation Army discipline. We are an Army, and we demand obedience."[3]

However, Brengle was sent "on trial" to a training school where his first assignment was to black the boots of eighteen other cadets! When he remembered that Jesus washed the feet of His disciples, his heart sang for joy. Never did he shrink from the humble quarters where he later found himself, the visitation routine, the every-night services, and the selling of the *War Cry*.

After six months' training, he returned, as Captain Brengle, to his native land where, with his wife, he labored for the salvation of sinners and the sanctification of the soldiers in the Army itself. "To insist upon holiness" wherever stationed was the passion of his heart, and for forty years his clarion call was heard all over the United States. His circle of influence widened to England, the Continent, and even to Australia, New Zealand, and the Hawaiian Islands.

A fellow-officer met Brengle at a railway station in California. So desirous was he for spiritual help that he could not wait for the first Convention service. "I want you for myself as well," he exclaimed. "I've read your writings, sensed your spirit, and I believe you can help me. I've grown a little dry in my own soul."[4]

This man and two other officers later engaged in daily prayer that Samuel Logan Brengle would be set aside by the Army for spiritual work only, that is for the building up of the spiritual life among officers and soldiers. They petitioned headquarters to this effect, and their request was granted. This recognition of Colonel Brengle as a prophet of God seems to have coincided with his own sense of call, for we find this entry in his diary: "And Samuel grew, and the Lord was with him, and did let none of his words fall to the ground. And all Israel from Dan even to Beersheba knew that Samuel was established to be a prophet of the Lord!" (1 Sam. 3:19, 20). What earthly honor or fame can compare with this! What dignity to be "a prophet of the Lord!"[5]

Brengle never dealt in generalities. Having seen the sin of his own heart, he knew what was in man. More than one hearer declared that Brengle preached directly at him. He was never guilty of making his congregation feel that they could in any way temporize with their submission to God. "Now is the day of salvation," he declared and, wherever he proclaimed the Gospel, the penitent forms saw many a spiritual victory.

As great as he was as a preacher, it is as a writer for which he will be longest remembered. He wrote only eight books, but it has been estimated that no less than a million copies have been printed in English and other languages as well. *Helps to Holiness* holds a very high place in its field and has been widely circulated to the spiritual enlightenment of thousands.

Birth-throes of agony often precede the production of that which is to bless multitudes. Enjoying his work in a certain town, Brengle received the startling message that he was appointed to No. 1 Boston Corps. He said later that a feeling of faintness came over him as he read the telegram, for this Corps was located in an extremely difficult area. Poverty, drink, and crime degraded the inhabitants among whom they would be working. Quiet for study and writing would seem impossible. What is more, the hall was not far from the Theological Institute and former fellow students would be visiting him in anything but enviable quarters. Boston spelled to him a living martyrdom. He prayed, "Lord, why do I feel this way? Am I proud? Is this appointment an offense to my pride? Am I not dead to these things?"

He then read the declaration of St. Paul, "I am ready not to be bound only, but also to die at Jerusalem for the name of the Lord

Jesus." He could not but exclaim, "Dear Lord, I too will be faithful. I am willing, not only to go to Boston and to suffer there if necessary, but I am willing even to die in Boston for Thee!"[6] Little did he foresee how near he would come to dying, nor could he know the blessed outcome to the spiritual interests of posterity.

The Brengles proceeded to Boston where blessing followed. And then one night, a drunkard, enraged because he had been ejected from the hall, hurled a paving brick which struck Brengle on the head. The devoted man hovered for some time between life and death and for eighteen months he was unable to preach. But fire such as had come upon Brengle's sacrifice could not be easily contained. The message of holiness burned in his bones. He wrote articles on the subject for the *War Cry* which were later collected and published under the title, *Helps to Holiness*. Mrs. Brengle later painted on the offensive missile the words of Joseph referring to his brothers' selling him as a slave: "As for you, ye thought evil against me; but God meant it unto good, to save much people alive."

Another of his useful books was the fruit of the distressing crisis which arose upon the secession of the Ballington Booths from the Salvation Army. To help keep the soldiers engaged in warfare for souls rather than in controversy, articles were written on the subject of soul-winning, which were eventually published as *Soul-Winner's Secret*.

Commissioner Brengle often was asked the secret of retaining the blessing of sanctification. Two years before his death he gave sound advice in answer to the query:

> Keep in the will of God, obey Him, seek Him daily, waiting at His gates. Read the Bible regularly. Never neglect secret prayer. Keep testifying to the grace bestowed upon you. Help others.
>
> I have been asked again if the realization of sanctification has ever waned during the past fifty years. Judging by my emotions, yes; judging by my volitions, no. There have been times when my emotional experience has ebbed out, and I wondered whether I had lost my Lord and my experience. Once I was sure I had, and I cast away my confidence, and for twenty-eight days was sorely tempted and sifted by the devil. When deliverance came—for I was not cast

away—I discovered that my will had not wavered in its purpose, that my volitions had held fast to Christ in the midst of the emotional storm and desolation that swept over my soul.

To all my tempted comrades, I would say: "Hold fast! Be faithful, regardless of how you feel, for Christ will never leave His own. He knows the way you take. He, too, was tempted for forty days and nights of the devil." That trial of faith and loyalty proved to be one of the greatest blessings of my life.

Sanctification has meant complete abandonment to the will of God, but not in such a way that my will has become passive in its functioning. It has had to be, and has been, active, firm, assertive in purpose to be the Lord's. I have not been allowed to sit in passive rapture singing myself away to everlasting bliss. God and man must cooperate, work together, both in the reception and continuance of the blessing.

The great heights are set over against the great depths. So the highest religious attainments are set over against the dark depths of fanaticism. And the only way to escape falling into that abyss is by being humble-minded and praying such a prayer as David's, "Teach me good judgment and knowledge." I have prayed for years that my light and my love might keep step with each other. Light without love may lead to pride—may make us supercilious and give us a false sense of superiority. Love without light may lead to great indiscretions and false judgments and fanaticism.

But we must beware of thinking that there is no further development. We are bidden to "grow in grace." We have entered into a rich grace through this act of sanctification, and we are to grow in it, though we cannot grow into it. We may, and should, increase daily in knowledge, in good judgment, in understanding, in ever-increasing love and devotion to God and to the well-being of our fellowmen. Jesus Himself grew in wisdom as He grew in stature and in truth.

We should forever get rid of the idea that sanctification is purely an emotional condition. It is equally volitional. You cannot, however, have any great inner experience without emotion. One of the greatest dangers to religion today is the fear, probably born of pride, that people have of emotion. They are so anxious to be balanced and well poised that they cease to be vital and natural. They become faultily faultless, icily regular, splendidly null—no more.

The highest religious experiences make men and women as natural as little children, and each one will express himself according to his own temperament. I would say to young people, "Don't be standardized. Be yourselves. Have some enthusiasm in your religion. Don't be a slave to what others may think. Keep your eyes off people and on Jesus and cultivate love for the people who try you. They may not always be wise, but if they are good, bear with them."

Some of my prayers I have not yet seen answered, but others that I poured forth with tears and strong desire for His glory and the salvation and sanctification of men fifty years ago are being answered before my eyes today in ways I did not, could not, foresee.

These fifty years have been rich in spiritual blessing and sweet fellowship with my Lord and His people. But they also have been years of toil, of temptation, of tribulation and sometimes of sore discipline of spirit amounting to agony. My Master is a Man with a cross, Who bade me take up my Cross and follow Him if I would be His disciple, learn of Him, and finally share His triumph.

In the year 1931, Commissioner Brengle retired from active service in the Salvation Army, though he continued to fulfill speaking engagements for at least two more years. Then declining health and failing eyesight brought about a curtailment, and finally, a cessation of public activity. On May 19, 1936, God called His servant to Himself.

QUOTATIONS BY SAMUEL LOGAN BRENGLE

One glad, sweet morning, God wrought mightily in my soul. All alone in my room, God revealed His Son in me. I was just as sure He had cleansed and filled me that moment, as I am that I am here now. I could not deny it any more than the man who was born blind could deny that Jesus had touched his eyes. I knew that, whereas I had been blind, I could see; whereas I had been impure, I was made clean.

You may pray with others, you may confess to others, but there will come a time when you will have to get alone with God, lost to everybody but God—though many be about you—as though there was no one but you and God in the universe.

I have seen His face in blessing
When my eyes were dimmed with tears;
I have felt His hand caressing
When my heart was torn by fears.
When the shadows gathered o'er me,
And the gloom fell deep as night,
In the darkness, just before me,
There were tokens of His light.

I have stepped in waves of sorrow
Till my soul was covered o'er;
I have dreaded oft the morrow
And the path which lay before.
But when sinking in my sadness,
I have felt His helping hand,
And ere daydawn came His gladness
With the courage to withstand.

I was wandering, and He found me,
Brought me from the verge of Hell;
I was bruisèd, and He bound me,
Sick was I, He made me well.
I was wounded, and He healed me
When a-wearied of the strife;
I was erring, and He sealed me,
Dead, His Spirit gave me life.

By His life's Blood He has claimed me
As a jewel in His sight;
As His own child He has named me,
Brought me forth to walk in light.
So I'm fighting till He calls me,
Walking in the path He trod;
And I care not what befalls me
Living in the life of God.

—S. L. Brengle.

Eva Von Winkler

MOTHER EVA OF FRIEDENSHORT

Eva fumed, and her pent-up rebellion found an escape as she climbed the roof of the neighboring house and shook her fist at the retreating figure of the cleric, muttering, "You shall not rob me of my liberty." Then, feeling most superior in her newly declared freedom, she jumped over the chimney stacks. She had just finished her second lesson preparatory to Confirmation, and she would be bound by no creeds.

Only two years before, the thirteen-year-old girl, usually obstinate, but now somewhat subdued and saddened by the loss of her mother whom she passionately loved, had uttered similar words. As she strode through the woods with her St. Bernard dog, she fancied that she saw the majestic and commanding figure of the Lord rising before her, and it seemed He wanted to "claim" her. "No! No! He shall not conquer me," she declared. "I will be free, and nobody shall take my freedom from me." Perhaps this young heiress of noble birth even then sensed the call of God to the service that was destined to bring blessing to thousands.

Eva von Winkler, next to the youngest of a family of nine boys and girls, was born in southeast Germany near the border of Poland, October 31, 1866. Their home, situated near the village of Miechowitz, was an ancestral castle and possessed all the charm and romance associated with such a place.

Eva's gentle, loving mother was, according to her daughter, "a radiant form of light." The memory to her children, not only of her unusual mental powers but also of her ardent, spiritual aspirations, proved to be an "imperishable inheritance" that enriched them as long as they lived. The father's contribution to his family was of a more earthy nature. A wealthy man, he wanted his children trained so that his estate, eventually to be theirs, would be handled by them with the utmost discretion. Consequently, he was a parent with strict ideas of discipline which he was not slow to enforce.

The mother's love for God was in evidence throughout the home. Nine chairs, each with a Bible verse carved on the back and arranged around a huge oak table, impressed upon formative minds the importance of God's Word. The inscription, "Quiet Approach to God," was written on the first page of the large family Bible. The famous book, *Imitation of Christ*, by Thomas à Kempis, was given a prominent place on the table.

Eva's first recollection of any spiritual desire was when two of her sisters sang a hymn, "Praise God Together, Ye Christians All." She remembered only once hearing about the death of Jesus when her Mother, who had been ill, told her the story of how Jesus had been nailed to the Cross for it was Good Friday. But apart from this one occasion, nothing was ever said to her about sin. As a result, it was long before the girl realized any need of a Savior.

When Eva was almost seventeen, the family went to Berlin, where they had a city home. Here she began to reach out after God.

> God Himself took me into His school. All that I had imagined I possessed lay crushed right to the ground. I had absolutely nothing— no ground under my feet, no future, no Heaven, no eternity, no God. Oh, how I searched night and day after the truth— and could not find it.
>
> What is life? What is death? What is time? What is eternity? These questions tormented my brain, but no answer came. Only now and again, a few words, which I must have read some time, came to me like a star in the night, although I scarcely knew Who had spoken them. "These things I have spoken unto you, that in me ye might have peace. In the world ye shall have tribulation; but be of good cheer; I have overcome the world." It was full of promise to me, and wonderful that Someone could say, "I have overcome the world." Who was this Person? I did not know Him.[1]

While engaged in Bible study, she read the tenth chapter of John with its beautiful description of the Good Shepherd. Her heart, now stripped of much of its rebellion, cried out, "Lord, if it be true that Thou art the Good Shepherd, then will I also belong to Thy flock." "Now," she tells us, "my heart was at rest; I had received the answer. This was the beginning of a new life. Everything was different in me and around me and, even though only the first rays of light penetrated into my dark heart, I still knew that the Lord had revealed Himself and that I belonged to Him from that time.[2]

Overtaken by an illness that confined her to bed, Eva began to while away the hours by a close application to the reading of the New Testament. As her newly awakened soul began to realize something of the cost of Calvary to the Son of God, His claims came home to her. She wrote:

> No longer did I need to spend my days uselessly and aimlessly; there was work for me to do in the world. Jesus Christ had sought me, found me, and called me into His service to follow Him, and now it only remained to wait for His instructions. . . .
>
> Then God gave me a friend in my loneliness. It was the old monk, Tauler from Strasbourg, whose sermons and additional writings I found when putting my mother's study in order. . . . Many an hour did this old friend of God talk there with the ignorant young child, of the union with God, through the death of our old self and the denial of the world and self-love.[3]

A steadily increasing desire was born in her to help all for whom Christ died. Assurance of God's plan was given, when several passages from the book of Isaiah were impressed upon her: "Is it not to deal thy bread to the hungry, and that thou bring the poor that are cast out to thy house? when thou seest the naked, that thou cover him?" Then followed words from the same prophet, "Also I heard the voice of the Lord, saying, Whom shall I send, and who will go for us? Then said I, Here am I; send me."

The once obstinate, determined Eva now tells us: "I vowed to give myself to His service exclusively, and begged Him to preserve me from all earthly love and keep me from all that might hinder me in my purpose."[4] Outwardly she maintained the same leisurely style of life, with much time on her hands. To prepare for the task ahead, she learned to knit, sew, took lessons in Polish, and read biographies. To discipline herself, she dispensed with her personal maid.

The path of usefulness which opened to her seemed quite insignificant. It was the custom at the castle to permit some of the neediest of the village poor to come at noon for a dish of soup made from bones, meat, and vegetables left over from the meals of the family. Eva began to serve it to them in the bowls they brought. When a small, half-starved boy came one day, she washed him, combed his hair, and decided later to make a pair of trousers for him from an old dress of hers. Soon after this, she met the mayor of the village and asked his help in aiding the child. Without Eva's knowledge, he presented the need to her father who became very angry. At the breakfast table the next morning, he scolded her roundly, forbidding her to go into the kitchen or even to speak to the villagers. Though brokenhearted at such restrictions, Eva began to rely more wholly upon God.

On her nineteenth birthday, she asked her father for permission to take a brief course in nursing. He consented on condition that a friend accompany her. And since the young Countess Lisa Zedlitz had the same desire, together they went to the town of Bielefeld, where there was a school in nursing and domestic arts. Pastor von Bodelschwing, whom Eva later called the "Apostle of Love," was in charge of the institution and she felt it "an unparalleled privilege" to be under his influence. His example of love to all, regardless of their station in life, was ever before her in after years.

On her return to her own home, she was permitted to invite eight small village girls to the castle to instruct them in needlework. One day, as she was fashioning a garment for the poor in her father's presence, he called her to his desk. At the same time, he turned to her oldest brother who also was in the room, saying, "If I should not live to be able to do it, build Eva a house for her poor people." The girl could only kiss his hand, and then she retired to her room to fall on her knees in a prayer of thanksgiving to God. At Christmas, great was her surprise to find that the gift from her father was the plan for just such a house.

Again Eva went to the institution at Bielefeld to learn how to conduct a household and, along with culinary and domestic training, she took charge of a small building for sick children. Soon after her course was completed, epidemics of scarlet fever, typhoid, and diphtheria ravaged the village, taking a fearful toll of young lives. So great was the strain imposed upon her from nursing the sick and burying the dead that, from sheer exhaustion, she was forced into temporary retirement.

During this time of recuperation, her house was in the process of being built. On the dedication day, Eva, at twenty-four years of age, was consecrated as its "Mother." So Friedenshort was established. Sick and crippled children were cared for; tiny babies occupied the wooden cradles; elderly persons, unwanted by their families, came for comfort and shelter. When the village school was ended for the day, fully a hundred youngsters came for help with their studies, training in wood carving, or in sewing, and for a period of fun and play.

Because of a limited income, Mother Eva made bread, did repair work, and raised cabbages, ever remembering and putting into practice the hymn sung at the dedication service, "And also in the hardest days, never complain about the burden." At the year's end, she had forty beds in the Home, instead of the five which had been there in its beginning.

In 1892, her friend, Pastor von Bodelschwing, visited Friedenshort and suggested that she start a Deaconess House, or Sisterhood, and train young women for various forms of Christian activity. The thought had occurred to her at various times, but her father's consent had to be obtained. "Little daughter, I have been watching you for a long time now and have seen that God's blessing rests on all you do," was his favorable reaction. Then he laid his hands on her head in fatherly benediction. So several new buildings were erected at Friedenshort, one for the incurably ill, and another for children. When these were dedicated, three young women were admitted as Deaconess trainees.

While Friedenshort was growing, the spiritual life of its mother also was being shaped and molded. She wrote:

> As time went on, there was much to discourage me. I remember in the early days, what a grief it was to find that my own village people mistook my wish to help them. Things were said which wounded me deeply, and then I would sit alone over my Bible and realize what it was to be hated by those one loves. As I turned the

leaves, my eye fell on the words, "If the world hate you, ye know that it hated me before it hated you." That was enough. Deep joy filled my heart, as I understood that His followers must not expect reward or thanks in this world which had rejected the One Who went about doing good.

Her assurance of the fact that she was a child of God never had been shaken. But, within herself, there were longings, vague and undefined, for a deeper spiritual life. For a long time, she was unawakened to the fact that holiness of heart was to be obtained by faith. She relied rather upon her good works to deliver her from the unrest of soul which at intervals proved so distressing. She even contemplated seeking an answer within the Roman Catholic Church. A letter written at this period reveals Mother Eva's heart struggle.

> Last summer I came for a short rest to "Salem," tired, worn out, discouraged, weak in body and soul. My whole work looked like a mountain of difficulties before me—a burden that I could not bear. In myself I saw nothing but sin, incapability, and weakness. I was almost too tired to speak or to eat. I took my Bible and went out. . . . I was able to have three days' quietness, and all at once a faint understanding dawned upon me of the meaning in the words, "My grace is sufficient for thee; for my strength is made perfect in weakness." That was the secret which had been lacking in my life. I always wanted to be something. I wanted to be holy, perfect, and glorious. I wanted to force it. Now a light struck me—I was to be just *nothing*—not even able to will or to do anything, so that Jesus and He alone should be all in all. . . . I look upon this as a new chapter in my life.[5]

Three saintly men were used of God in the further instructing and fashioning of His servant. One was Pastor von Bodelschwing, who had done much to train her for leadership during the years she spent under his guidance. His confidence in her strengthened and matured her. But the strenuous work in the institution, aggravated by the deep inner conflict of her soul, brought physical problems. While in Bielefeld, she saw the danger of absorption in Christian work to the exclusion of the deeper spiritual life. The sermons of Dr. Tauler had created a thirst for union with God and holiness of heart. But Pastor von Bodelschwing, failing to understand her quest, assured her that the answer to her need was not to be found in the Evangelical Church.

The second person to be of help at this period of her life was a small man, Fritz Oetsbach, deformed in body, but strong in the grace of God, whom Mother Eva met at a Faith Conference in May, 1900. She saw in him the indwelling Christ. His prayers opened Heaven. After seventeen years in a hopelessly crippled condition, he read in the Bible the words of the apostle, James 5:14-16, and asked Christian friends to pray for him, anointing him with oil. His obedience to the divine command was rewarded, and he was healed. When Mother Eva was privileged to engage him in conversation, he asked, "Have you ever thought that the word, 'There remaineth therefore a rest to the people of God,' is even now for you?" Eva tells of her astonishment at such a question:

> I looked at him in amazement. No, I had never thought of that. Life seemed to me a continuous struggle against my own nature, against the powers of sin and Satan—how was it possible to think of rest? Then the little "great man". . . spoke so simply, so clearly, so convincingly how this rest was meant to be for us here, as soon as we cease from our own works and enter into the rest of faith, which Christ won for us on the Cross, and into which we can enter, through the fellowship of His death. . . .
>
> Oh, how often I had longed for rest, had thought to find it only in the seclusion of a convent and inexorable asceticism or, if even not there, then only in the grave. And now this little man spoke not only of the possibility of rest even here, but he himself seemed to possess this rest—and indeed something of this divine rest actually proceeded from his personality.[6]

His words made a lasting impression upon Eva, and she always referred to Fritz Oetsbach as the "Apostle of Faith."

In the same year, her life touched that of James Hudson Taylor, whom she termed the "Apostle of Sanctification." From Mrs. Taylor she received a small book entitled "A Holy Life and How to Live It." In a simple way, it answered many of her questions in regard to holiness.

The work at Friedenshort was extremely arduous. Her pastoral friend, von Bodelschwing, following her activities with keenest interest, confided to the Sisters that she could live probably only another five years without a change of environment. The Homes were placed in other hands, and she became the Lady Superintendent of the Bielefeld Institution. Here, to be sure, her spiritual influence found wider scope in training others, but here also, willing to become an integral part of something entirely apart from the work she loved so much, she buried her ambition for Friedenshort in the tomb of her heart. But, within six years, a complete physical breakdown necessitated a removal to Switzerland.

Returning eventually to the beloved establishment she had founded, she chose to live in a cottage on the grounds, delegating the superintendency of the Community to an older deaconess. She devoted herself to the poor, and in her little home found a place for small waifs whose brief years had known nothing but cruelty and neglect. But her soul remained unsatisfied.

> The goal had been shown to me, but I had not yet reached it. The great gift of God, a holy life lived in the power of the Holy Spirit, which others were enjoying, I had not yet realized. Struggling, striving, fighting, I was always painfully conscious that I was not rising to God's ideals in my life. Neither outward poverty nor the daily opportunity for loving service could silence the tumult in my soul, and often a deep sigh arose from my heart, "Is this all? Has God nothing more to give me?"[7]

However, the time was fast approaching when the yet unfathomed depths of her being were to be reached by the immensity of the love of God. In the early part of the twentieth century, a marvelous work of the Holy Spirit took place in Wales. Eva, with friends, journeyed first to England and then to Wales. While in London she visited Bethshan, Mrs. Elizabeth Baxter's home for spiritual healing. Of this time she wrote:

> I had been allowed a glimpse into Mrs. Baxter's life of priestly intercession. My own life was so full of work, of unrest and strife, and there was so little time for prayer and worship. About this, too, she was tremen-

dously in earnest and said, "How can your spiritual life prosper when you spend no time before God?"...

During those days in London, another thing also happened which was full of meaning for me. Mrs. Penn-Lewis was then at the beginning of her spiritual ministry and, through her writings and her special witness to the meaning of the Cross, was exercising a great influence over a wide circle of Christians. A short conversation with her gave me light on the deepest need of my life. The old "I," which thrust its way into everything—even into the service of God and which, through no strength of my own, could be uprooted and overcome—I saw for the first time had been judged already in the Cross of Christ when He died for me. I saw this, but could not yet grasp it.

Then we passed on to Wales where the revival had just broken out. . . . The impression that we received of the unconquerable power of the Holy Ghost over a whole neighborhood was tremendous.[8]

As she traveled back to London by train, three young girls were in the compartment with her. Their worldly dress suggested to Mother Eva that attendance at the revival services would benefit them. When they told her they were singing and witnessing in association with Evan Roberts, the young man so mightily used of God in the revival, she was astonished. She asked herself the following question:

Was it possible that these girls in their worldly clothes, just as you see them on the streets in the great cities--*these* girls should be used of God to help in revival meetings—used to save souls when perhaps they themselves were only just converted from a life of worldliness and vanity—and now, instruments in God's hand? And I? For years I had been working in the Lord's service in simple clothes, denying myself everything in the way of comfort and outward attractions, and yet I was inwardly so poor, so weak, and so barren.[9]

As she pondered and drew out her Bible, her eyes fell on those verses: "For ye see your calling, brethren, how that not many wise men after the flesh, not many noble, are called: but God hath chosen the foolish things of the world to confound the wise; and God hath chosen the weak things of the world to confound the things which are mighty; and base things of the world, and things which are despised, hath God chosen, yea, and things which are not, to bring to naught things that are: that no flesh should glory in his presence." "The longer I thought about it," she writes, "the more clearly I saw that God could more easily use a shoeblack from the London streets than He could use me. What I had formerly looked upon as an advantage appeared to me now as a hindrance."[10]

These same young women were scheduled to hold a service in a Welsh chapel near London and Mother Eva, as a humble learner, decided to attend. She could understand very little of the language, but the Holy Spirit was present as Teacher. She wrote:

> It is something unspeakably wonderful when God Himself comes down into a gathering and touches each, speaks to each personally. Then everything high and lifted up must bend before Him. All hardness breaks down, all coldness melts. To meet with God, the Unseen, to realize His presence in deed and in truth, is the greatest, highest, most wonderful experience that men can ever know. He can then in one moment give and accomplish that which we, in long years of our own striving have never been able to reach. In that hour, there came to me a gentle, heart-searching question from my crucified Lord, "Are you ready to be a fool for My sake?"
>
> In that hour also the old life sank into the grave—something new, until then unknown, was given. My soul's longing was satisfied. It seemed to me that all my soul travail was left behind and that now He Himself was living in me—Christ in me, a new I, a new life. . . . Only one wish remained, one longing, never to be disobedient to Him, Who had afresh taken possession of my life. No more I, but He through me from now on. In that same hour, the purpose came to me to travel back to the homeland and witness to Christ in the house of near relatives. That was no easy road.[11]

Upon her return to Friedenshort, Mother Eva gathered the Sisters together, asking pardon for "all that had been my own, self-born and self-planned, in my previous service amongst them. From henceforth, all must be different; no more I, but He." The Holy Spirit broke down all self-righteousness, and divine forgiveness, assurance and newness of spiritual life, for the first time, came to some of the Sisters. Between the years, 1905 and 1908, fifty Deaconesses were housed in the rapidly growing establishment, and the problem of finances became acute. The interest on Mother Eva's inheritance, the legacy of her mother, no longer was sufficient to meet the expenses, nor could the endowment fund legally be resorted to. She saw then that the work must be conducted on the principle of faith which had been adopted by George Müller, Hudson Taylor, and others less widely known. This produced some degree of misunderstanding with her Committee. After much prayer, she issued a statement, written by herself, which resulted in the resignation of all her former Committee. She was then free to choose only those in sympathy with her complete trust in God.

However, her faith was sorely tried. Poor health again had forced her into retirement. During her absence of eighteen months, the expenses of the Homes exceeded the income. But, in answer to united prayer, within six weeks the last vestige of indebtedness was removed and a substantial amount left over. On scriptural grounds, debts were never again incurred at Friedenshort.

In the latter part of 1910, the need of a shelter for homeless children in Breslau, Germany, was laid upon her heart. The initial gift for the purpose was the small sum of five marks. She laid it on a chair and, kneeling, asked God that it be multiplied as had been the loaves and fishes for the feeding of the five thousand. Within a few weeks, a lovely home on a beautiful estate near Breslau came into her hands. During the next fourteen years, forty shelters were opened in various parts of Germany and Poland. It was no small joy to Mother Eva that, after the opposition of her family in early years, a brother and sister each established a "Home for the Homeless" and gave themselves to God and His service.

Divine blessing rested upon the labors of His devoted servant, and the sphere of usefulness, opened to the Deaconesses, widened. In 1912, several Sisters were assigned to an area in China with the C.I.M., where no European woman ever had ventured. Upon the heart of a Norwegian Deaconess was laid the spiritual destitution of the fisher folk of Lapland. Before Mother Eva's death, Sisters were working in Guatemala, Syria, Africa, and India.

Another avenue of service was that of prison visitation. Eventually a home was opened where discharged prisoners were permitted to live until adjustments could be made to normal life.

The shadows of evening at length fell over Mother Eva's beautiful life. In an effort to prolong her days, those who loved her recommended the bracing mountain air of Switzerland. But it proved to be of no avail, and she was removed to the little cottage at Friedenshort, to await the Master's call to higher service. In June, 1932, the "earthly house" was dissolved, and she entered into one "not made with hands, eternal in the heavens."

The books, still in circulation, that flowed from her pen, point out clearly and beautifully the path to holiness and Heaven.

QUOTATIONS BY SISTER EVA

Wherever God has found any who, in singleness of heart, have humbly yielded themselves to Him to obey, and to follow simply wherever the light of truth may lead, He has made them light-bearers and witnesses, each according to the measure of his gifts and the sphere of his influence, and has used them to be a blessing to others. They may have differed radically from one another in their doctrinal views and convictions, they may have been influenced by their surroundings, the leadership they followed, and the particular tendency of their time, yet each has given expression to some ray of revealed truth through his words and works, and their life and witness has been a means of blessing not only to their own generation, but to those who have followed.

When the Holy Spirit has entered into possession of a life, every moment that follows must be a renewed receiving.

Many a restless, defeated life would be transformed if it became a life of prayer. Prayer costs something. It costs much! He who would pray must deny himself. He must give his whole time and strength to the service of God. That does not mean he must change his outward calling and become "spiritual" by entering so-called Christian work. No, to serve God is to live for God and glorify Him, to be at His disposal and forget oneself in seeking His glory and the salvation and good of mankind.

The world holds the right opinion that there can be no such thing as a worldly Christian. Every man is either a child of the world, governed by the spirit of the age, fighting the battle of existence in the kingdom of this world, thinking, acting, living according to its principle, or he is a Christian, a follower of Jesus Christ, gripped by an inflexible determination to see His words and commandments realized in action and in life, even if they should mean to him what they meant to his Lord—rejection and death!

Samuel Morris

ANGEL IN EBONY

In the early hours of the morning, a wife, hearing her husband's footsteps, expectantly opened the door to welcome him after his long hours of labor in mission work in New York City. She could not conceal her surprise, when she saw with him a shabbily clad youth of the African race. "Who is this, Stephen?" she queried in a most expressive tone. "An angel in ebony," he replied, at the same time escorting the lad into the hallway of his comfortable home. The man of the house was none other than Stephen Merritt, a good Methodist minister and home secretary to Bishop William Taylor.

The boy was Samuel Morris, who through strange and miraculous ways and by God's guidance alone, had been brought from the African bush to the crowded city of New York and from the depths of paganism to the heights of divine grace. And no more fit appellation than that of "angel in ebony" could have been given him.

Kaboo, an African prince, was born in the Ivory Coast in 1872. His father, a petty chieftain, became involved in several tribal wars. It was the custom at that time for the oldest son of the vanquished chief to be taken by the conquering tribe and retained until payment of the war indemnity. Should it be deferred, the unfortunate hostage was subject to physical torture of the most brutal type. Care was taken that the father of the pawn be notified of the punishment.

Kaboo was first carried away when a small child. The tribute was brought promptly, so he was returned to his home. The second time the boy was held for several years. He never talked of the dreadful treatment he had received, apparently trying to erase it from his memory. On the third occasion of his father's defeat, the victors were headed by a brutal savage whose ability to devise cruel and ingenious forms of torture would seem to have been almost unparalleled. Fifteen-year-old Kaboo was carried away captive and, as soon as possible, ivory, nuts, rubber, and sundry articles were brought to the conqueror. Though accepted, it was not enough for the ransom, so with aching hearts, the people of the boy's village parted with everything possible to redeem him. In addition to quite a varied cargo of goods, the father, fearing that the youth would die under prolonged torture, decided to offer one of his daughters in exchange for his son. The amount brought was declared still insufficient and Kaboo, knowing the fate that awaited his sister, refused to return to his home.

Since no further indemnity seemed to be in the offing, Kaboo was given a daily beating. Each time the punishment was more severe, and the thorny poison vine used reduced his back to shreds of torn bleeding flesh. When the boy would be unable either to sit or stand, the fiendish plan was that he be laid over a cross tree and beaten into unconsciousness. The next form of torture was to be a burial to the neck. His mouth, kept open by an inserted stick, would be smeared with something sweet. This would attract ants and cause the most exquisite pain. Driver-ants, which consume human flesh, would then be permitted to do their worst, and Kaboo's skeleton was to be placed where all defaulters could view it and be suitably warned.

What happened after the youth was placed upon the cross tree can be explained only by the fact that there is a God in Heaven Who can, when He so wills, exert His power on man's behalf. Kaboo afterward said that a bright Light appeared, enveloping his bleeding form, and a Voice, also heard by those around, told him to flee. With the command, came the ability to obey, though his natural strength was almost depleted.

He found shelter in a tree hollow until darkness settled down upon the jungle. With the coming of day, a "kindly Light" illuminated his path and, by its aid, he was led for a matter of weeks, he knew not where. During this time, he was guarded from wild beasts and poisonous serpents, as well as from cannibals who inhabited the tropical forests. Nuts and fruit provided sustenance, and one never-to-be-forgotten day he found himself on a plantation outside Monrovia, the capital of Liberia. Here Kaboo found employment.

It was on a Friday that he had escaped from his would-be murderers, and it was on the same day of the week that he reached the one place in Liberia where the laws of civilization were enforced and he was safe. From that time, every Friday, his "Deliverance Day," he abstained from both food and drink.

On Sunday, Kaboo attended church and heard the account of the conversion of the apostle Paul. As the missionary, through an interpreter, spoke of the Light that shone about him on the Damascus road, the lad exclaimed, "I have seen that Light! It is the same Light that brought me here." The missionary, Miss Knolls, a graduate of a Christian college in the United States, only recently had come to Liberia, and her prayerful interest in the attentive African youth before long was rewarded by his entrance into the Kingdom of God. He became a humble learner at the feet of Jesus and showed daily evidence of a divine touch upon his life.

It was not long, however, before Kaboo became awakened to the need of a still greater change. His dark past had left desires for revenge upon those who had so cruelly tortured him. He yearned for deliverance from innate and nameless fears. Hungering and thirsting for more of God, after his day's toil, he would spend much time in prayer. His companions in the small quarters where he slept failed to understand the deep longings that caused him at times to break out in supplication to God, and he was forced into the woods to talk to his heavenly Father.

Late one night, he returned to his bed, his heart still lifted in prayer when, he said later:

> All at once my room grew light. At first, I thought the sun was rising, but the others were sound asleep. The room grew lighter, until it was filled with glory. The burden of my heart suddenly disappeared, and I was filled with a sense of inner joy. My body felt as light as a feather. I was filled with a power that made me feel I could almost fly. I could not contain my joy, but shouted until everyone in the barracks was awakened. There was no more sleep that night. Some thought I had gone crazy; others, that a devil had gotten into me. . . . I was now a son of the heavenly King. I knew then that my Father had saved me for a purpose and that He would work with me.

Kaboo by no means understood the theology of what had taken place. But, in response to deep longings after God, a complete commitment to Him, and his simple faith, the Holy Spirit had come to this unlettered, ignorant African boy in such power that the lives touched by his saintly and almost other-world influence are more than can be numbered.

He became a member of the Methodist Church in Monrovia and was baptized under the name of Samuel Morris. It was chosen by Miss Knolls in a gesture of gratitude to an American banker of that name who, during missionary training years, had assisted her financially. Samuel spent two happy years in Monrovia, supporting himself by doing odd jobs. Miss Knolls and others gave him lessons in English and reading, and he proved to be an apt pupil.

By a most peculiar and yet providential coincidence, his path crossed that of a young slave boy who had witnessed his torture as a pawn. He had escaped from his master and made his way to Monrovia. Through Samuel's influence, the lad was led to Christ and baptized under the name of Henry O'Neil. He, too, had seen the Light that shone around Kaboo on the cross-tree and had heard the Voice that bade him rise and flee. The youths became fast friends, as well as worthy ambassadors of the Lord Jesus.

One of the missionaries, recognizing Sammy's potential for spiritual leadership, advised him to go to the United States for further education, so that eventually he could be a greater help to his own people.

As the matter was engaging the boy's thoughts, someone read to him the fourteenth chapter of John's Gospel, where Christ told His disciples of the future coming of the Spirit of God to the world. This was the first occasion that what he himself had experienced in the plantation bunk house was defined. For hours at a time, the lad pondered the subject and went from missionary to missionary in Monrovia, asking questions about the Holy Spirit. Finally, one friend, unable to answer his queries further, said that most of her knowledge had been gleaned from Stephen Merritt of New York City.

"I will go to New York to see him," declared Sammy.

As soon as he could, he walked to the seacoast where a sailing vessel was anchored in the harbor. When the captain came ashore in a small boat to bargain about the cargo to be assembled, great was his astonishment upon being confronted by a young native, who greeted him with the words, "My Father in Heaven told me you would take me to New York. I want to see Stephen Merritt who lives there."

"You are crazy, boy," was the captain's rejoinder, turning away with an oath.

He came to the shore several times, and on each occasion Sammy repeated his plea. Before the scheduled sailing, however, the captain was forced to replace some deserters. The lad approached him again with the confident assertion, "My Father told me you will take me now."

"How much shall I pay you?"

"Nothing. Just take me to New York, so I can see Stephen Merritt." And so Sammy Morris began another chapter of his book of life.

As he boarded the vessel, he saw a youth lying on the deck, unable to walk because of an injury. Sammy knelt at his side, asking God to heal him. At once the prayer was answered. The captain had supposed that the boy he had taken aboard was an experienced sailor and, when he learned otherwise, was about to send him ashore. "Please keep him. He has done so much for me," pleaded the lad for whom prayer had been answered.

Consent was gruffly given but, as occasion offered, the captain rained cuffs and blows on him, as well as on the crew, who presented the most ungodly array of men that could be imagined. A veritable giant, a Malay, whom everyone feared, took an especial dislike to Sammy, vowing to kill him. During a drunken brawl, the Malay, cutlass in hand, was advancing on some of his shipmates, when Sammy quietly stepped in front of him with the words, "Don't kill! Don't kill!" A strange power seized the half-crazed man and, dropping his weapon, he retired to his bunk.

Hearing the commotion, the captain appeared, ready to shoot the miscreants but when he saw that Sammy had stopped the fighting, followed him below deck. As the lad knelt and prayed for all on board, the Holy Spirit sent a shaft of conviction to the heart of the wicked man and, kneeling, probably for the first time in his life, he thanked God for sending this boy among them. His whole manner of life was renovated. Rum no longer was distributed to the crew; fighting gave way to prayer services and to Sammy's singing of the old Gospel hymns that never fail to reach the heart. When the Malay was stricken with an illness that seemed fatal, Sammy's prayers were answered in his restoration to health. The boy he had hated then became the object of his devotion.

When the ship reached New York after nearly six months at sea, the crew provided Sammy with clothing. Though by no means the best, it enabled him to go ashore fully clad. The parting with his friends, for that was what these rough sailors had become, was painful, and many wept as they bade the lad good-bye. This humble, Spirit-filled boy, by his influence and prayers, had opened their eyes to a higher plane of living than they ever had believed possible. Some of them became true penitents at Calvary's Cross.

It was on a Friday that the ship was docked and, as Sammy set foot on American soil, he called out to the first person he saw, "Where can I find Stephen Merritt?"

The tramp, for so he was, had attended a city mission where he had met that gentleman and knew exactly where to find him. "I'll take you to him for a dollar," he offered. After a long walk, Sammy and his companion reached Mr. Merritt's office as he was locking the door to leave for the day.

"I am Samuel Morris. I have just come from Africa to talk with you about the Holy Spirit," was the lad's greeting. Mr. Merritt conducted the youth to the Mission next door to his office, promising to see him later.

"I want my dollar," called out the tramp, who had been completely forgotten in the strange meeting.

"Stephen Merritt pays my bills," replied Sammy. And his newly-found friend smilingly handed the guide his fee.

After attending to some business, Mr. Merritt returned to the Mission. He never forgot the sight that greeted him. Seventeen men on their knees, with tears streaming down their cheeks, were humble suppliants for God's mercy. Sammy stood in their midst, his dusky face aglow with the light of Heaven. At the conclusion of the service, Mr. Merritt took the boy to his own home, where he gave him the bedroom reserved for the Bishop when he came to New York. The surroundings were so bewildering to the African lad that Mr. Merritt, much to his own amusement and enjoyment, had to help him prepare for the night. At breakfast the next morning, Sammy, having had no food since Thursday evening, did full justice to Mrs. Merritt's culinary skill.

It was Mr. Merritt's duty that day to officiate at a funeral, and he decided to take his young guest along. Two other ministers were to assist and to ride to the service in his carriage. The sight of a poorly-clad black boy in the coach of the home secretary of the Bishop was startling in the extreme, and they climbed into the carriage with a reluctance they could not hide. To relieve his own embarrassment and to put his friends at ease as they drove along, Mr. Merritt pointed out to Sammy various places of importance in the metropolis. But the interest of the youth in these wonders was slight and, suddenly turning to his host, he questioned, "Have you ever prayed in a coach?" No, he had never done so, was the admission. Sammy's biographer tells us what followed:

> "We will pray," said the lad and, as Mr. Merritt stopped the horses and knelt, Sammy talked to God after this fashion: "Father, I wanted to see Stephen Merritt, so I could talk to him about the Holy Ghost. He shows me the harbor, the churches, the banks, and other large buildings, but says nothing to me about this Spirit I want to know more about. Fill him with Thyself, so that he will not think, talk, write, or preach about anything else."

In all the former years of his religious life, never had the presence of the Holy Spirit been so real to Stephen Merritt, as when this African youth, his soul aflame with the love of God, prayed for him in such untoward surroundings. From that time, he was a changed man, and his ministerial friends caught a vision of holiness they never before had seen.

When they proposed to buy clothing for Sammy, they thought the best was none too good for this "angel in ebony." Never had such a sermon poured forth from the lips of Stephen Merritt, as the one he delivered at the service that day. So powerful was the movement of the Holy Spirit that many persons knelt at the casket, repenting of spiritual deflection.

In view of the lad's purpose in coming to America, Mr. Merritt decided that Taylor University, then located in Fort Wayne, Indiana, would be the place where Sammy could best receive a Christian education. He recommended him to the school authorities as "a diamond in the rough."

On Sunday, the boy accompanied Mr. Merritt to a Sunday School and was asked to talk about the Holy Spirit. The mirth of the scholars when the African youth mounted the platform was soon changed to weeping, as the presence of God came into the group. A "Sammy Morris Missionary Society" was formed, which made itself responsible for clothing, books, and other things the boy would need at the College. Three trunks of gifts resulted.

Within a few days, Sammy was on his way to Fort Wayne, which he reached on Friday, his "Deliverance Day." Dr. Reade, the college president, asked him if he had any preference as to living quarters. "If there is a room nobody else wants, give it to me," was the reply.

Dr. Reade, writing to a friend, said, "I turned away, for my eyes were full of tears. I was asking myself whether I was willing to take what nobody else wanted. In my experience as a teacher, I have had occasion to assign rooms to more than a thousand students. Most of them were noble Christian young ladies and gentlemen, but Sammy Morris was the only one of them who ever said, 'If there is a room nobody else wants, give it to me.'"

The College was in the throes of a financial struggle, and an appeal was made for funds to educate the lad who had come from the west coast of Africa to learn about the Holy Spirit. The response was disappointing, until a butcher, Josiah Kichler, donated five dollars for what he termed the "Faith Fund." This act and name suggested a way to arouse interest in Sammy's education and, when the "Faith Fund" was advertised as such, money was given in ever increasing amounts.

One day the boy asked Dr. Reade if he might secure employment. "I want to earn money so that Henry O'Neil can come here to be educated. He is a much better boy than I. He worked with me for Jesus in Liberia."

It was decided that they pray about the matter, and the next day, Sammy, face wreathed in smiles, exclaimed, "Henry O'Neil is coming soon my Father tells me." Within a short time, Dr. Reade was informed that a missionary who had known both boys in Africa, had returned to America and was arranging for Henry's education in the United States.

Sammy's schooling posed serious problems, for what he had learned in Monrovia had been extremely elementary. He required special teachers, but the matter was settled when several young Christian women assumed the responsibility.

The Sunday after his arrival at the College, Sammy learned of a church for African Americans in Fort Wayne. He set out to attend it, but it was so far he reached it late. Introducing himself as Samuel Morris who had just come from Africa, he astounded the minister by saying he had a message for the congregation. That gentleman, about to discount such an unusual statement, was restrained, however, by the glow of Heaven on the boy's face. He said later that, although he did not remember a word of what had been said, he felt the presence of the Holy Spirit as never before. The entire congregation went to its knees, some weeping over their sins, and others rejoicing at what God was doing in their midst.

The results of such a revival could not be hidden, and the local newspapers made known to a wide area the name of Sammy Morris, the young African attending Taylor University. Many persons came from far and near to visit him. Always courteous but not interested in mere chitchat, he handed each caller a Bible, with the request that a portion be read aloud. In this way, he hid the Word of God in his heart.

A student in the College with atheistic principles, thinking he could confound the African lad by his arguments, asked for a personal confrontation with Sammy. When he came into his presence, the boy in accordance with his usual custom, handed him the Bible, requesting that he read a chapter. The older man instead threw the Book on the table, saying scornfully, "I never read that Book any more, for I don't believe a word it says."

Sammy, astounded, was silent for a few minutes. Then, the tears coursing down his cheeks, he asked incredulously, "My dear brother, when your father speaks to you, do you not believe Him? When your brother speaks, do you not believe what He says? The sun shines, and do you not believe it? God is your Father, Jesus is your Brother, and the Holy Spirit is your Sun. Kneel down and let me pray for you."

The Spirit of God smote the heart of the proud man and, before the end of the term, he was converted and eventually became a Bishop.

During Sammy's career at the College, the financial situation became most acute, and it seemed the school must be closed. Interested persons felt this could not take place with such a Spirit-filled student as Sammy Morris in attendance. And the "Faith Fund" saved the College. So many donations were given that the trustees were able to purchase ten acres of ground for a new school in Upland, Indiana. And there Taylor University stands today, a memorial to the young student from Africa who exemplified to his generation and all succeeding ones the possibilities and power of God's grace.

Sammy loved the country that had taken him to its heart. The changing seasons were sources of enchantment and gratitude. He interpreted the falling snowflakes as messages from Heaven and once in prayer fervently exclaimed, "A year here is worth a lifetime in Africa."

But the winters of the United States proved too rigorous for this child of the tropics, and a severe cold weakened his naturally frail constitution. He continued to attend classes and church services, but the fact that he was ill could not be concealed. He was taken to a hospital in Fort Wayne, where loving care did all possible for the "angel in ebony."

At first, Sammy did not understand why prayer for his healing was unanswered. But when his heavenly Father tenderly revealed to him the fact that soon he would be in the City where "the inhabitant shall not say, I am sick," he accepted with joy the knowledge that the purpose of God in his life had been fulfilled. In May, 1893, quietly and peacefully, he fell asleep in Jesus.

But death did not end all. Although the youth himself never reached his native land, other hands than his carried the Gospel torch into its darkness. At a prayer gathering soon after Sammy had passed away, a young man said, "I must go to Africa in his place. It is my prayer that the mantle of his simple faith will be thrown over me." At the same time, two others volunteered their services.

The influence of Sammy's life continued to act as ripples on the lives of many he had contacted. The atheist student who had been converted during college years, had entered the ministry and, while conversing with a radical unbeliever, the latter became so angry that he struck a blow which felled the clergyman into unconsciousness. Normally, with returning senses, he would have been retaliatory. Instead, however, came a vision of Sammy, under the blows of the drunken sea captain, praying him into the Kingdom of God. "If Samuel Morris could forgive that man," he said, "cannot I have the same spirit?" Struggling to his knees, he lifted his voice in prayer, with the result that the atheist soon was asking forgiveness for his display of temper and crying to God for mercy on such a sinner as he.

Several years after Sammy's death, the captain who had brought him to America visited Stephen Merritt. When he heard that his young friend was in Heaven, he burst into tears, saying that most of the sailors who had known the lad were still manning the ship, and that his saintly influence had brought about permanent transformations among them.

After his brief contact with Sammy, Stephen Merritt himself entered into a new era of spiritual life. In a ministry among the mentally disturbed, he was especially blessed, many healings resulting in answer to his prayers.

Sammy's last resting place in Linden Wood Cemetery in Fort Wayne, Indiana, has become a "Mecca" for many of both the white and black races. The sacred influence of the Holy Spirit seems to linger around the spot, and conversions there have not been unusual.

To any who doubt the validity of the remarkable incidents in the life of the "angel in ebony," the words of Dr. Reade are worthy of thought: "Most of us have gone too far away from the simple faith of childhood, and God cannot do many mighty works in us because of our unbelief."

GOD IS WORKING OUT HIS PURPOSE

Through men whom worldlings count as fools,
    Chosen of God, and not of man,
Reared in Thy secret training-schools,
    Moves forward Thine eternal plan.

And now, though hidden from our ken,
    In Midian desert, Sinai's hill,
Spirit of God, Thou hast Thy men
    Waiting Thy time to do Thy will.

When blazing out upon our night
    Flashes the Pentecostal flame,
May I be found with heart alight,
    Burning to magnify Thy Name.

Not as Thy prophets who declare
    The Word that thousands hear and own,
I only want the smallest share
    In setting Christ upon His throne.
              —*Bishop Frank Houghton.*

Iva Vennard

DEDICATED EDUCATOR

The camp meeting at Normal was a time of great reunion, and Iva Durham attended the opening day, chiefly for the sake of meeting friends. Among them was an old acquaintance, Joseph H. Smith, who greeted her warmly. Then, in a rather abrupt manner, the man of God unburdened his heart. "I'm glad to see you here, Miss Iva, but I'm afraid I shall have to say that I have been increasingly disappointed in you. When I knew you a few years ago, I thought you were one young woman who was going to be spiritual, and more than that—a spiritual leader. But I see you seem to have gone mostly 'to top.'"

This blunt statement of fact set Iva immediately on the defensive. At the same time, it once more awakened within her the old dissatisfaction of soul, for she knew that her faithful friend had spoken the truth. Eventually, after a fierce struggle with pride and ambition, the young woman made a complete surrender to her Lord. Indeed, from that time onward, she became so abandoned to the will of her heavenly Father that when, once more, a friend made an appraisal of her Christian character, she could honestly say that Iva Durham Vennard, "ranked high among the King's daughters. Her queenly dignity, sanctified ability, sound judgment and rare quality of leadership were a benediction."

Iva was born in the state of Illinois, U.S.A., in 1871. Her father, a northern soldier, survived the horrors of the Civil War, only to die of tuberculosis several years later, leaving his wife with three daughters and an adopted son. Mr. Durham had won the respect of his neighbors by his godly life. As long as he was able, he visited various homes in the town, offering prayer. Mrs. Durham possessed a strong Christian character and rose bravely above the loss of her husband, supporting her family by the profits accrued from a dressmaking and milliner's shop, as well as a photographer's studio. Within a few years after the death of her husband and that of her oldest daughter, Ione, she moved to Normal, Illinois, in order to be near a brother.

171

Iva, then only small, had been deeply impressed by the last testimony of her sister. She was not converted, however, until she was twelve, when she attended a series of children's services held in the town. As she advanced into the teens, her spiritual progress became retarded by the social life into which she was drawn. When she enrolled for teacher's training at the University of Illinois in Normal, she permitted her studies to crowd out the warmth of her "first love" for the Savior. Then, too, her closest girl friend was the daughter of a Unitarian minister who, because of Iva's beautiful voice, occasionally invited her to sing in his church. As the association grew more intimate, she began to read Unitarian literature and, before long, suddenly realized she had become engulfed in a sea of doubt in regard to the truths of God's Word.

It was in the summer of her nineteenth year that she had first met Joseph H. Smith. Although she told herself she knew she would be bored and consequently took along some of her skeptical reading material, Iva had agreed to attend, with her mother, a camp-meeting at Decatur, Illinois. Among those in charge at the camp were two godly men, J. A. Wood, author of *Perfect Love*, and the other, that man of God mentioned above, who later figured so prominently in Iva's spiritual life. As the services progressed with the presence of the Holy Spirit in evidence, the girl became so conscious of her need that she burst into tears and made her way forward for prayer, remaining until she received an assurance of divine pardon.

In the autumn of the same year, Iva was again moved by God's Spirit during meetings held by Joseph Smith. It was then that she claimed the experience of entire sanctification as far as she understood it. It was then, too, that she volunteered for missionary work in Japan but, a year later, was unable to pass the necessary medical test on account of her history of tuberculosis. Thus Iva was forced to lay aside all plans for foreign service and to continue with her teacher training at Normal.

At its completion, Iva plunged wholeheartedly into her chosen profession. Once more this talented young woman was drawn into the vortex of worldliness. In fact, for the next two years, she so far laid aside her religious convictions as to indulge in card-playing and even yielded to the allurements of the theater and opera. The education she had acquired created a thirst for more and, in the autumn of 1892, she enrolled at Wellesley College for girls.

Ida's charming personality and the bent of her intelligent mind had interested the professor of modern languages at the Normal University. When he was made president of Swarthmore College near Philadelphia and invited Iva to spend the Christmas holidays with his family, she happily consented.

Thus, of this year at Wellesley, Iva writes, "It was one of the greatest years of my life culturally though in my heart I was not submitted to God."

This great spiritual unrest continued during the following year which found her teaching in California. In turmoil of soul, one Sunday she attended a Methodist Church in Santa Ana, where, to her astonishment, the minister that day was J. A. Wood. His sermon on the words, "Blessed are the pure in heart: for they shall see God," brought back floods of memories of better days spiritually. Once again Iva turned to Bible study, and prayer too became a reality.

With her return to Normal, however, worldly ambitions again became uppermost. Her professor friend now hoped she would complete her college course at Swarthmore and promised to secure a scholarship for her. He himself intended eventually to accept a professorship in a German university and suggested that Iva accompany him and his family to Europe, making her home with them. Then she could attend lecture courses at Oxford and, in the summer holidays, study French and German. The future beckoned with rosy fingers to the talented young woman and, all things considered, she decided to go to Swarthmore.

But, since God's ways are not man's, Iva's plans came to a decided halt. It was at this juncture that she had attended the Normal camp-meeting, met her old friend Joseph Smith, and found herself in the throes of a great struggle. Iva was brought to a realization of the fact that she was consulting only her selfish desires in regard to the pattern of her life; she was giving no place to God. In vain, she argued with the relentless Holy Spirit, "But an education is not wrong; it is not carnal to desire to be intellectual. God gave us our minds, and He wants us to use them."[1]

After days and nights of agonizing prayer, but with an increasing longing for a sense of divine favor, she said "Yes" to God's question, "Will you forever put the spiritual before the intellectual?" And Swarthmore, with its promise of worldly advantage, was erased from her future.

Having thus decided, it now remained for Iva to face her professor friend and tell him of her change of plans. He happened to be visiting in Normal at the time, and so, with the scholarship certificate in her hand, she approached him with much agitation. "I must return the scholarship," she confessed. "I cannot go to Swarthmore this year." Both astonished and grieved, the professor exclaimed, "You make me feel as though I were attending a funeral."

"You are," was the rejoinder, "my funeral." Then, hoping he would understand, she added, "I've made my choice to be spiritual first, and that means my unswerving allegiance to Christ in every detail."

To her great astonishment, her friend replied in a most kindly manner, "I would so much rather you would be a noble woman than a great scholar."[2]

Scarcely able to control her emotions, Iva rushed home and, throwing herself across her bed, gave way to a flood of tears. She said later that life never looked so desolate as when she accepted the Cross with its death to self. In desperation she cried, "Oh, God, I must hear from Thee." Reaching for her Bible, she opened it. The words in Isaiah 60:1, "Arise, shine; for thy light is come, and the glory of the Lord is risen upon thee," seemed to leap from the page. At once, a wonderful sense of inward purity gave her the assurance that God had, without a shadow of doubt, accepted her sacrifice, and her empty heart became filled with unutterable peace.

It was then that she discovered the secret burden her dear mother had been carrying on her behalf. Now, while tears of joy flowed down her cheeks, Mrs. Durham exclaimed, "God has answered prayer! He will show you what the next step is to be."[3]

While waiting for this "next step" to be made clear, Iva began to accept calls, first to sing and then to preach, in an aid to revival efforts in various churches. In one village, it turned out that she was the sole evangelistic party. "Men came from the river bottoms, barefooted, with guns in their hip pockets," she relates. "It was a far cry from Wellesley and the New England Conservatory, but my heart was at rest through it all."[4]

Thus, throughout those early days, the Holy Spirit unctionized her message and many were converted. Iva became more and more convinced that definite Christian service was to be God's will for her life. At the same time, however, she balked at the thought that preaching was to feature largely in her ministry. In the first place, she disapproved of women preachers. Then, too, the Methodist Church at that time, did not ordain women for preaching and, as she put it, she had no desire for a "nondescript ministry under no particular auspices, and with no denominational recognition." And so, while she earnestly prayed for guidance, she had a secret hope that "He would excuse me from preaching, and let me be perhaps a singer or a social worker."

That summer it so happened that a friend, the superintendent of a deaconess home in Buffalo, New York, visited Normal and asked Iva to consider returning with her to her post of duty. The girl became sure of God's plan when He impressed upon her the words of the prophet Isaiah, "If thou draw out thy soul to the hungry, and satisfy the afflicted soul; then shall thy light rise in obscurity, and thy darkness be as the noonday." Perhaps, too, there was the comforting thought that, in this sphere of work, God would not require her to preach. Be that as it may, He saw her sincere desire to serve Him and was willing to wait a little before revealing His full plan for her life.

So, about a year after the blessed reality of her encounter with God, she arrived in Buffalo, with an appointment as field representative to Conference Evangelism. She adopted the deaconess garb, with the bonnet and white silk ties, which indeed proved extremely useful in her night visits to city missions, and, even in church circles, she found it spared her from social involvements which could otherwise have absorbed much of her time.

This period of Christian service, however, was not without its problems. This Methodist Conference was not loyal to the doctrine of sanctification which Iva believed and had experienced. Some of the pastors she was called upon to assist were drifting from the old-fashioned standards of Methodism and did not wish again to revert to the "old paths." In deep distress of soul she would pray, "O Lord, please let me go to Japan or Africa, or anywhere rather than this burned-over territory, among this prejudiced and stiff-necked people." It pleased God, however, not to answer this cry of her heart—at least, not for the time being. So Iva continued, midst many hardships, in her deaconess work. In her travels, she lodged in accommodations often poorly heated. The monthly allowance for deaconesses in the Methodist Church was only eight dollars, and she accepted the position of trusting God alone for personal needs.

In January, 1896, she assisted in revival services in a wealthy church. Her travail of soul was such that, during her three weeks' stay, she was not able to stand in the pulpit without first taking refreshment. But the God-given burden was not in vain, for a well-to-do lady in the town opened her heart to the young deaconess and, after prayer, became converted. Turning completely from her selfish life, Lavinia Parish, until her translation to Heaven, gave of her abundance to Iva for three and one half years. Her lovely home was a haven of refuge, and her thoughtful care in providing well-cooked meals and warm clothing enabled the young servant of Christ to fulfill her God-appointed tasks. When, because of physical problems, Iva was forced into a sanatorium for treatment and rest, Miss Parish assumed all expenses.

In the spring of 1898, Iva was appointed Deaconess-at-large. This meant that her duties took her all over the United States, where she opened training institutes for deaconesses, gave addresses at Epworth League convocations, and performed other such duties. But she realized to an increasing extent that church organization and politics were taking the place of active evangelism. After a day of fasting and prayer to God for a revelation of His will in regard to the matter, divine guidance came in the promise, "I will make my words in thy mouth fire" (Jer. 5:14), and in the Scripture, "Many . . . believed on him for the saying of the woman" (John 4:39). "I laughed aloud," she tells us, "and the cloud lifted." After years of doing evangelism, Iva had at last come to realize that she was actually called to it. This being the case, she determined to take her stand.

But her choice brought much personal suffering and misunderstanding. Consulting the Secretary of the Women's Home Missionary Society who controlled the Deaconess Order in regard to inserting a course in evangelism into training, she met with a courteous but definite refusal. What was she to do next? An answer came through the suggestion of Bishop Thoburn: "You found a training school yourself with this special evangelistic curriculum." Then he continued, "This is an answer to the prayers of my sister Isabella in India. She has been asking God to save the Deaconess Order and to make it a soul-winning agency." Advising her to express her opinions in a letter to the board of bishops, he promised personally to deliver it.

Thus it was that, in October, 1901, Iva received permission to open such a school in the city of St. Louis, Missouri. The next year, the "Epworth Evangelistic Institute" came into being, and for eight years it continued with encouragement from the bishops, but with mounting prejudice and opposition on the part of minor officials who were embracing more liberal views than those upon which the Methodist Church was founded. Iva Durham became shocked at "the cruel unfairness and heart estrangement that could develop among Christians." But she had received a commission from her Lord and she kept faithfully on with her training of young women, keeping before them constantly the wonderful work that the Holy Spirit was able to accomplish in their lives, when they were wholly submitted to Him. After some setbacks, the most spiritual of teachers were found, which gave Miss Durham more time to engage in the evangelistic work that was ever dear to her heart.

Meanwhile, Iva had met the man who was eventually to become her faithful partner. Tom Vennard, an architect and mason contractor, had agreed to wait ten years if necessary for his bride while she established the work at Epworth. Iva, although admitting that, if she were to marry anyone, it would be he, held out little hope of there ever being a possibility of marriage, knowing the demands upon time and strength made by the work to which God had called her.

But Mr. Vennard had told her that he firmly believed the time would come when she would need him. "And then you will find me waiting," he had said.

After much prayer and fasting, Iva received comfort through the promise in Jeremiah 32:39, "And I will give them one heart, and one way, that they may fear me for ever, for the good of them, and of their children after them." She became assured that some day, God would open up the way for marriage, and when that time came, her ministry would be enriched.

That time came perhaps sooner than either of them had anticipated. After two years of waiting, the couple were married and embarked upon twenty-six years of partnership, blessed of God, and made possible because of the husband's unselfish attitude towards his wife's life of public ministry. "I am willing to be your background of support," he had pledged in their courting days, and he had meant it.

After nearly five years of married life, God blessed the Vennards with a baby boy. For a while, however, it looked as if neither mother nor son would live. But after a period of anxious waiting, it became apparent that both were to be spared, in answer to much prayer. It was some time before Mrs. Vennard could resume her former responsibilities and, when she did, it was to find that practically all responsibility, except that of raising finance, had been taken out of her hands. Textbooks, courses of study, in fact nearly every detail had been changed. "Methodist preachers do not want deaconesses who study theology," she was told. "If our deaconesses are trained in theology, they will become critical of the preachers, and that will be the end of the deaconess movement."

Heartbroken, Iva Vennard felt that her time at Epworth had come to an end. She had been termed by some as "a dangerous and powerful woman," and it was evident that those in authority were afraid of the influence she wielded and were determined to render that influence void. Thus in October 1909, she offered her resignation to her board of trustees. "You are angular in your positions, Mrs. Vennard," they told her. "You have not learned how to compromise." But Iva stuck to her convictions, and when told that "these epochal experiences were outmoded and that the new method of reaching people would be religious education," she replied:

> I understand the issue, and it is because I have already made my choice that I am now presenting my resignation. I also understand the tendency of modernism, and I have made my choice to remain with orthodox Methodism. I believe that the two epochal experiences in grace are Scriptural. I have sought them, and I believe I have entered into both. Such realities of Christian experience can never become out-of-date.[5]

Thus, at length, they were forced to accept her resignation. Mrs. Vennard told her friends:

> We shall never cease to praise God for these eight beautiful years we have enjoyed at Epworth. He has owned our labor with His gracious favor in the pardoning and purifying of multitudes, and in the sending forth of young women prepared to labor, with the fullness of the blessing of the Gospel of peace. . . . Now God leads us and we are going with the note of triumph in our soul.[6]

Some time before, Mrs. Vennard had received an invitation from the Christian Witness Company in Chicago to start a training school there. It would have its own charter, and, though a branch of the National Holiness Association, would be completely independent. She would not, however, take so vital a step without consulting her husband. She suggested that perhaps she should not take on the responsibility of another such institution. Instead, they could have their own home, while she still engaged in evangelistic work during the summer. His answer was clear and firm. "No, Iva. . . . You are still too young to give up this training school work, for that has come to be your real call. Your evangelistic work is merely contributory to it. If we thought only of our selfish preference now, we would soon lose our assurance of the Lord's favor. And if we backslid, we would both be unhappy, and our home would not have the right atmosphere in which to nurture our son. For his sake, as well as our own, I want you to go on."[7]

And so Iva Vennard accepted the invitation. In the meantime, that summer proved to be especially blessed of God when, at a camp-meeting, her ministry was particularly fruitful among the young people. She felt this to be a seal upon the step she was about to take. Then, too, a rich personal blessing came to her at that time. The preacher every morning spoke from the text, "Ye shall receive power." She tells us in her own words what followed.

> One of the most deeply spiritual and most mystical experiences of my life came to me while he was preaching on "power to suffer." I was in the midst of persecution. Tongues were clamoring. A persistent propaganda was being circulated that I was leaving the Methodist Church and going over to the Nazarenes, and that I was trying to turn Methodist money and students, through C.E.I., to that denomination. With all this load on my heart, I needed a special lift from God, and it came on that morning.[8]

She was especially strengthened at that time by Job 23:10, "But he knoweth the way that I take: when he hath tried me, I shall come forth as gold."

That Mrs. Vennard needed this time of spiritual strengthening God alone knew, for the coming days were not to be easy ones for her. During the busy months of preparation for the opening of the new school, a calamity fell upon the entire holiness work in Chicago. The treasurer of the Board of Trustees of the Chicago Evangelistic Institute, as the new venture came to be called, died suddenly. Mrs. Vennard felt it keenly, for he had been one whose vision for the school had been the clearest. Then, in addition, the gentleman who was to have been the Dean of Men, accepted another position and, without these two on whom she had relied for strength, she felt completely stranded. The words, "Be strong and of good courage, and do it . . ." were of great encouragement to her. "No one," she tells us, "has ever guessed how much I craved a human arm to lean upon at this time, but God kept me shut off from such support."

Throughout those early years of the new Institute, Iva Vennard went through many difficult periods. Of one such crisis she writes:

In my panic my faith ceased to function. This was a desert place for my soul. In November there was a revival service at the First Nazarene Church. . . . My Friend, Professor Yates, began singing to his own accompaniment, "I will Pour Water on Him That Is Thirsty." An old, old song, but how the Spirit of the living God applied it to my soul. I began to weep. The terrible numbness of my spirit was melted, and my faith once more took hold.[9]

Thus she continued to stand firm to her God-given convictions. Even those who did not fully agree with her had to admit that they never knew a woman with so much courage. As her biographer puts it, "Out of these bitter months she learned anew that no group is perfect, irrespective of what label it may wear. Even among the Lord's people, selfishness is selfishness; bigotry is still bigotry, and fair-mindedness and loyalty are jewels all too rare."[10]

But God did take her through these difficult years in triumph. He also gave her some stalwart friends to help her in the work. Yet God was the only One to Whom she could fully unburden her aching heart. At times she would shut herself away and wait until new strength was received. During one such experience, the Lord said to her, "Can you not trust My love? If you prove faithful in this fiery trial, I will make you a blessing to your students, and your living will testify to the reality of holiness more than all your teaching"

Out of a bleeding heart she answered, "My Father, it is absolutely committed to Thee. I'll wait until the Judgment Day for my vindication, if that is Thy will."[11]

This was perhaps one of the most outstanding spiritual qualities that this godly woman possessed. She had learned from God's school never to resort to self-vindication. Not that it was always easy to wait in patient trust for God's timing in the matter. For it was not until 1937 that Iva felt that at last, the chill winds of criticism and entrenched unfriendliness towards the C.E.I. were beginning to abate. By this time, she was a widow, having lost her faithful husband seven years earlier. This had indeed been a great loss, made no easier by the fact that it came in the difficult years of the depression when financial ruin threatened the Institute.

By this time, too, she had become Dr. Vennard, having been given the degree of Doctor of Divinity by Taylor University in 1923. To her students, however, she had remained the same warmhearted, spiritual counselor and mother. This tribute was indeed typical of the cordial affection and respect held by many who had been under her tuition. "Her messages were always a challenge to 'our utmost for His highest.' . . . Her purity of heart and life, her devotion to God and to the work to which He had called her, her perfect love toward God and her fellow men, have been a lodestar throughout my life, and I shall ever praise the Lord for His love in permitting me to know one of the great saints of our day," said one.

At last, strength began to fail and, in 1945, Dr. Vennard received her call Home. The last years had been brighter ones for her. Her son and two adopted daughters were happily married and progressing spiritually. Her many children in the Lord surrounded her with love and grateful affection and, above all, her friendship with her Master had grown stronger and closer as, one by one, her faithful friends of former days had left her for their heavenly Home.

Now she was about to follow in their steps. Her last word was indicative of her many years of implicit trust in the will of her Father. Now she was about to enter His presence forever—about to leave her beloved work in His hands. As she entered the gates of Heaven, the one word she had so oft repeated while traveling here on earth, she uttered for the last time as she breathed her last. And that word? It was one simple, fervent, heartfelt "AMEN."

The great mistake of most persons in seeking for a deeper spiritual life is the attempt to become something themselves and have something which they can call their own holiness. On the contrary. God is ever seeking to withdraw us from ourselves, to lead us to realize our helplessness and nothingness, and to find our all in Himself continually and forevermore.—*A. B. Simpson.*

"The meek will he guide" (Psa. 25:9). Be content to lose the idea of thine own importance; cease to be wrapped up in the contemplation of thine own claims and rights. Be not counting on honors to be rendered thee, hour by hour, from this man and from that. Give up the vain idea that every hour owes thee an ample tribute of manifold benefits. Shrink into non-importance and take the position of a simple servitor, whose business it is to do, to suffer, and to give thanks.

When you have become thus inconsiderable in your own regard, and have relinquished the honor which cometh from man, and are cordially willing that the gifts that adorn this present life should be withheld from you, and abundantly bestowed at your right hand and at your left; then will you become conscious that another hand is locked in yours, a friendly hand, a gracious hand, a tender, considerate, careful hand, a royal, heavenly, nay, without disguise, a Divine hand. In surrendering all self-importance, you have become unspeakably important to the most exalted Being in the universe. You have entered the very path trodden by the Lord Jesus Christ. In that path you walk with God,

The secret of habitual meekness is the love of God habitually shed abroad in the heart. All pride, all avidity of worldly good, all insubmission, imply a grossly inadequate idea of the value of Christ's love. Thou canst disdain the riches that take wings, in the consciousness of unseen wealth—untold, imperishable.—*George Bowen.*

Johanna Veenstra

A FLAME FOR GOD

A golden-haired, blue-eyed girl, overwhelmed by awe and confusion, stood at the bed of her beloved father as he talked of meeting his Savior in Heaven. For only seven months, he had served as the pastor of a Christian Reformed Church in the state of Michigan, U.S.A., when he succumbed to an attack of typhoid fever. Life was not the same after this to Johanna Veenstra, and she became a source of anxiety to her widowed mother. Often in school she was disobedient and rebellious, and so insubordinate a scholar was she in the Sunday School that her teachers were forced to expel her.

Johanna had come into the world in 1894, in Paterson, New Jersey, U.S.A., in a Dutch community, said to have produced more workers for God according to its population, than any other part of the city. Between the ages of fifteen and sixteen, she secured a position as typist in New York. With a delightful sense of freedom and money of her own, she yielded to an increasing love of the world and its pleasures. She purchased dresses of the latest fashion, with accessories of jewelry. She began to frequent the theater and was about to also indulge in the dance, when she was peremptorily and startlingly arrested by the voice of God in the single word, "Stop!"

About to conclude the day's work in the office, Johanna was summoned to the telephone. She recognized the voice of her minister, asking her to come to his home that evening. Much to her own surprise, for at that period of life she had no desire for religion, she thanked him and accepted the invitation. When she reached the doorstep of the parsonage, though she scarcely knew why, she was trembling most violently. His fatherly, kindly manner put her at ease, however, and his evident concern for her soul brought her to tears and, after a time of prayer, she bade him good-night.

That visit meant a turning point in her gay and thoughtless existence. For almost a year, she lived more or less under a sense of a burden of sin. After the day's work, she often slipped away from the rest of the family to pray. One evening, her sister, curious to know what she was doing, peered through the keyhole of the door of the bedroom to which she had retired and saw the girl on her knees. Johanna frequently was unable to sleep, gripped with a dreadful fear of death and Hell.

At length came a divine revelation, convincing her that the reason she could not find rest of soul was that she was not submitted to God and His will. In other words, she had sought relief from the guilt of sin and had desired the joy such relief would be sure to bring, but she had wanted this without the price of complete surrender. The struggle that followed was most poignant. But when Johanna looked up to Heaven, exclaiming through her tears, "Anything, Lord," her heart was at once eased of its load, and an assurance of pardon was hers.

Her life no longer was a giddy pursuit for pleasure, but rather one of service to God. Until she was nineteen years of age, she found great happiness assisting Mr. Peter Stam of the "Star of Hope Mission" in Paterson several nights a week as well as on Saturday afternoons. He was the father of John Stam who, with his wife Betty, suffered martyrdom in China in 1934. John, however, was but a child at the time Johanna was a helper in the Mission.

When the young woman entered the Union Missionary Training Home in Brooklyn, New York, she was not at all certain that full-time Gospel service was God's plan. For three weeks after enrollment, Johanna could not bring herself to unpack her trunk. But all doubt was removed when the words of Jesus were impressed upon her, "No man, having put his hand to the plow, and looking back, is fit for the kingdom of God."

During her second year at the school, she represented the students at a Missionary Conference in Lake Geneva, Wisconsin. One of the speakers was Dr. Karl Kumm, brother-in-law to Geraldine Taylor, well-known author for the China Inland Mission. In a large area of Central Africa, he had not met a single missionary of the Cross and was greatly burdened for the evangelization of its numerous heathen tribes.

Johanna listened to Dr. Kumm's address with breathless interest. As he depicted the condition of scores of dusky African tribes dying outside the pale of the Gospel, her heart was moved. At the close of the service, she retired to her tent where she spent three days alone in communion with God. Then she knew that, in "the heart of the Eternal," her field of service was to be Nigeria.

Johanna was not permitted, however, to go to the African field until she was twenty-five. So the next three years were spent in training for midwifery and in work with a city mission that acquainted her with almost every conceivable type of Gospel effort. She took the message of the Cross to rescue homes, prisons, hospitals, gypsy camps, and even into the houses of ill-fame and opium dens in Chinatown of New York City.

In October, 1919, she said good-bye to her native land. An unforeseen delay in passage detained her in England for three months but, in the early part of 1920, she reached Lagos, formerly reputed to be the largest slave depot on the western coast of the "Dark Continent."

But before she reached her appointed station in Central Africa, a long journey awaited her. At Ibi, welcomed by the Field Secretary of the Sudan Interior Mission, she was told that her final assignment was to be the Takum district where, among cannibals, the Mission hoped soon to gain a foothold for the Gospel. It was more than a year before she reached the place of her designated labor. But the time was not wasted for, in the interval, she gained such a command of the Hausa language that, in six months, she was able to preach in that tongue.

During this period also, Johanna reached the most important crisis of her life, one which ever after set her apart from ordinary Christians. Spending much time in prayer, she was led by the Holy Spirit to a clearer comprehension of His work upon the human heart. She read and reread and read again two books on His work and witness which created in her an intense hunger to be crucified with Christ. Eva Stuart Watt, her biographer, said of this search:

Then she saw that the work she had come to do was not hers at all, but the Holy Spirit's. He had been sent from Heaven to reveal Jesus to the hearts of men. All He needed were instruments willing to be used. She could preach to the heathen for a lifetime and preach well, but never convince one of them. She could wear herself out working and yet reap no harvest. HE came to convince of sin. HE came to do the reaping. Would she allow Him to break her and empty her and then to work through her? Eternity and eternity only will tell the sacred value of those lonely evenings with God. Johanna later confided to a fellow-missionary the blessing God gave her through the challenge of those books. It meant nothing less than her complete abandonment to the Holy Ghost and His coming in to dwell in her heart.

The Holy Spirit had introduced Johanna to the place that lies within the veil, and she said never an hour passed but that she was conscious of the immediate presence of God. A friend wrote of her: "I'm convinced that the inner closet was the secret of her success as a missionary. It was this frequent and oft converse with her Lord that made her so confident on the battle front." She had learned her own nothingness and henceforth drew upon her inexhaustible supplies in Christ. "The flickering self-life" was extinguished by "the blaze" of God's glory, and Johanna could say with St. Paul, "The world is crucified unto me, and I unto the world."

In February, 1921, Johanna set out for her desired haven. With porters to carry the baggage, her means of transport was a bicycle. The area to which she was assigned was in view of the Cameroon Mountains, and included many small villages in the foothills where the Prince of Darkness apparently reigned. Demon-worship was prevalent, and the blood of frequent human sacrifices seemed to call to Heaven for vengeance. Child marriages and polygamy were the usual thing. One chief was said to have had ninety-three wives. She wrote home:

I won't dwell on the darkness. I couldn't if I tried, but sometimes—I say it solemnly—sometimes I have felt as if I were being drawn through the very gateway of Hell itself. . . . I do so want to learn the lesson of letting the Lord carry the burdens for me—not just because that is the easiest way, but because it is His choice. I am so slow to learn these precious lessons.

Prayer was her solace and strength. The routine of the day's work, with household planning, morning services for the native help, classes for the children of the nearby villages, frequent calls for medical aid—all was preceded by secret prayer for an hour or more. Before dawn, Johanna would spend time meditating, a small hurricane lamp shedding its light on God's Word. In the stillness of that morning watch, she caught a glimpse of the Almightiness of the Lord of Hosts and she knew He was on the battlefield with her. Her biographer writes:

> She was very conscious of her weakness and unworthiness, but determined that He should conquer in her life. She believed in the Senior-partnership of the Holy Ghost. He knew the country to be taken, and though stone walls or giants defied her, He was equal for all. If she spent time enough in His presence, He would reveal His plans to her. Only in implicit obedience to His commands, she knew, could victory be expected. So, like Joshua, she would fall down before the Captain of the host and say, "What saith my Lord unto His servant?" And she was yielded to follow His leading, even though it often crossed her own inclinations.

When the battle raged strong and Satan seemed to triumph over the souls of those she had watched over, she would keep a night's vigil. Prayer to her was spiritual warfare. She could wage a relentless battle against the powers of darkness with these spiritual weapons. This worker trained souls to be spiritual warriors like herself. One little widow was known to the villagers as "The Daughter of Prayer." In the prayer meetings she would supplicate the Throne with tears running down her cheeks for the ones who had grown cold toward the Lord she loved. Sometimes the body of this intercessor would be bent to the earth, her face buried in her clasped hands. She prayed aloud morning, noon, and night for the surrounding tribes and missionary stations. Although unable to read a word of the Bible, yet she was learned in the heavenly art of taking spoils from the enemy by prevailing prayer.

Saturday was always a sacred preparation day for the Sabbath. Nothing was allowed to interfere with this time alone with the Lord. Even the most tantalizing mail from home would be laid aside until Monday if it should arrive on Saturday, and visitors were asked not to make their calls at the weekends.

In the course of her years of service, Johanna was aided from time to time by helpers from other stations, all agreeing that she was a superior missionary. A colleague on the station with her said: "She was GREAT, very humble, very human. If she was ever irritated or offhand with me, through tiredness, she would always come in the evening and say, 'Forgive me for being cross today.' Prayer cemented us. Morning and night we prayed over everything."

This valiant soldier was asked to visit Donga where the field bristled with difficulties. In a letter Johanna wrote:

> Mr. Hood's last remark to me about the work before he went home was, "The stench of Donga reaches to Heaven," and I believe it is true. Donga for some time has been at low water mark spiritually and has been going back rather than forward. It was with hesitation and trembling that I was willing to come here at all. Mr. Hood had told me of the many tangles.

The Wednesday prayer-meeting, her first service after her arrival, was most depressing and the behavior of the people most frivolous. A special session with the Christians was arranged at which time she told them some home truths. With tears she urged repentance, assailing their secret sins and reproving them for their treatment of former missionaries. She told them she had counted the cost of their hatred of her for thus speaking God's message. The response was brokenness and confession of sin as one after another arose to tell of disobedience and wrongdoing. Nineteen were suspended from church membership. Again she wrote:

> If beer-drinking is a bar to taking the Sunday service then there is only one man in Donga eligible. May God help me to straighten things here. After all, speaking to a crowd is comparatively easy compared to dealing with one nominal Christian on the sensitive

point of his stinginess in never sparing a copper for the Lord's work. It is easy to read in Church, "Thou shall not steal"; much harder personally to tackle one you know is dealing dishonestly. We are not brazen enough in our stand for righteousness or fearless enough in our battle against sin.

The leader at Donga was dismissed and replaced by four other Christians. The chief, though a professing Christian, had been tampering with witchcraft and was playing a double game. God had given Johanna favor with him and the courage to boldly denounce his duplicity. Much prayer ascended to Heaven, and convicting power descended upon the chief, resulting in his seeing things he never before had understood. Johanna wrote home:

> Donga is to be pitied. Satan knows where to attack. Oh the pathos of it all! They need more help. After four weeks with them, we leave next Tuesday. I feel the month has been well worth while. Let's not grow weary or faint. The battle is His and the victory sure.
>
> If the Spirit of God would only convict us of the value of New Testament methods and help us to put them into practice! We may pray and weep and fast for the rest of our lives, but, unless we obey the Lord, we shall never have blessing. He is jealous. Oh, that He might write His law on our hearts.

As the warrior missionary walked on with God, she learned how trifling with sin, either in one's own personal life or in the lives of the converts, only results in confusion and deadness. At a missionary conference, she shared with her fellow-missionaries the truths she had been learning:

> In talking about Church discipline with one of our workers, the remark was made, "Why be so exacting, demanding more of these Christians than is done at home?" Never must we attempt to compare the Church on the mission field with the Church at home in its degeneracy.
>
> The New Testament explicitly commands discipline. Most of us are unfaithful, not because we are unconvinced of the need in the Church, but because we shirk what is without doubt the most difficult part of our work on the field. It cannot be done unless we

have God's Holy Spirit. We need discernment, and who but the Holy Ghost can impart this? We need courage to deal with sin before a holy God, and who but the Holy Spirit can give such courage? We need consolation for our own hearts and love for the one who has defiled the Church of Christ. Only the Spirit can give these gifts.

How is it that Satan can keep sin hidden in the bosom of the Church year after year without our knowledge? Because we lack the wisdom from above to discern it. One Sunday morning, I was taking the service and speaking on the text, "Know ye not that your body is the temple of the Holy Ghost?" While speaking, the Spirit of God convinced me that the one sitting immediately in front of me was guilty of immorality. I was talking at the time about the seventh commandment.

I returned home. This man (being my cook at the time) came to me for orders. My whole being rebelled against having to speak to him, but I managed somehow to say, "Sit down. I have a question to ask you." I put it to him. Was he guilty?

"Yes, Baturiya," he exclaimed at once. "Who told you?"

It was difficult to make him believe that no one but the Lord Himself had told me. The truth all came out. The sin had been committed only two days previously. A missionary took exception to my action, saying we had no right to suspect our Christians. I ask, "Was it suspicion that gave Peter boldness to drag to light the sin of Ananias and Sapphira, or was it revealed by God?"

We need to see sin, too, as God sees it. I am inclined to think that many of us have a very unscriptural judgment of sin. For instance, here is a member of the Church guilty of vice. The news of his sin travels from Dan to Beersheba. With one voice, the Christians everywhere believe that he should be censured and barred from communion. I agree with them. But here is the difficulty. Another member, greedy of gain, stays away from worship on Sunday and engages in his trade. The lust for money has gripped his soul, but he is not censured. The first defiled his own body, the second, God's holy day.

We do need courage. In the Bible Training School, I chose as my life motto, "Only be strong and of a good courage." Little did I realize then how much I would have to lay hold of this commission. This courage is not mustered by will power. It must be given from above. Never shall I forget when I had to rebuke a teacher evangelist. He had been with the Mission a long time. I was keen to keep him, but he was getting very slack. It took three weeks of prayer before I had the courage to call him up. It would have been so much easier to carry on and say nothing. Only the Holy Spirit can give us courage to crucify personal feelings and follow His conviction.

No one can exercise discipline in the Church and not find his own spirit wounded. Often the offender shows resentment. Some time ago a baptized Christian left his firstborn to be reared in the home of a Mohammedan relative. I wrote to the father, showing how he had despised the precious gift God had given him, that if God took the gift away he was not to murmur. Two months later the child died from burns received in that Moslem home. The father was bitter. No doubt he thought I had bewitched the child. Shortly afterwards he wrote me a letter, in which he cursed my father and my mother and the day of my birth. I read the letter. I prayed for courage. Next day I called to see him, but he was not at home. Then came furlough. Two years later, under cover of darkness, the bereaved father came to me and asked me to forgive him.

If we are true to our calling in the matter of discipline, God will give the comfort of His Spirit. Never yet has anyone said a really unkind word, but they have returned sooner or later to apologize. God perfects all that concerns us and His work. But discipline must be in love. However fierce the struggle in dealing with sin, love will always triumph. Constant prayer will keep the love-fire burning in our hearts.

It was Johanna's conviction that the African churches should, as soon as was practical, become indigenous. For the highest good of the African, she imposed upon herself a rule "never to give anything without payment, except the message of priceless redemption."

And so she toiled on amid sunshine and shadow, firmly believing that the Gospel seed, sown in tears, would produce a harvest of joy. She writes: "When I see the devoted love to the Lord Jesus in some of these Africans and their childlike trust in Him, I have often thought—I say it reverently—that in the Kingdom of God I shall not feel worthy to sit at their feet."

In December, 1932, despite several furloughs to the homeland, her wearied body demanded rest. She planned in the Spring to spend a month in a higher altitude but, before doing so, consulted a doctor in regard to a nagging pain she could not diagnose. The verdict was that an operation for appendicitis would solve the problem. Though it was successfully performed, suddenly, April 8, 1933, at only thirty-nine years of age, Johanna felt herself sinking and called for assistance.

To those around her, it was evident that the sun of her life was setting, and she knew it too. As prayer was offered at her bedside, she exclaimed, "Altogether lovely! Altogether lovely! He's my portion." Then, sending a message to the Church, as well as to her mother, she uttered words of triumph, never to be forgotten by her friends: "I'm not sorry. It is all in the will of God. I couldn't have chosen anything better than to go like this. I'm all unworthy, only a sinner saved by grace. Thrown into the presence of the Lord! Jesus, Victor over death!"

Remember God's rule—all for all. Give Him all. He will give you all. Consecration avails nothing unless it means presenting yourself as a living sacrifice to do nothing but the will of God. The vow of entire obedience is the entrance fee for him who would be enrolled by no assistant teacher, but by Christ Himself, in the school of obedience.—*Andrew Murray.*

The consecrated, one-talent man or woman has promise of a larger influence for good than any intellectual genius who has not met the Master.—*Samuel M. Zwemer.*

Notes to Sources

1. Nicholas of Basle

1. Frances Bevan, *Three Friends of God*, (London: James Nisbet & Co., 1887) pp. 268-269
2. Ibid., pp. 224-226
3. Ibid., p. 227
4. Ibid., pp. 238-239

2. John Tauler

1. Frances Bevan, *Three Friends of God*, (London: James Nisbet & Co., 1887) p. 7
2. Ibid., p. 15
3. Ibid., p. 18
4. Ibid., pp. 18-19
5. Ibid., p. 56
6. Ibid., p. 61
7. Ibid., p. 68
8. Ibid., p. 69
9. Ibid., p. 214

3. Christmas Evans

1. B.A. Ramsbottom, *Christmas Evans*, (Luton: The Bunyan Press, 1985) p. 10
2. Ibid., p. 14
3. Rev.Paxton Hood, *Christmas Evans*, (London: Hodder & Stoughton, 1881) pp. 44-45
4. Ibid., pp. 52-53
5. Ibid., pp. 55-56
6. Ibid., p. 56
7. Ibid., pp. 56-59
8. Ibid., pp. 71-72
9. Ibid., pp. 76-78
10. Ibid., pp. 78-81
11. Ibid., p. 81
12. Ibid., pp. 155-156
13. Ibid., pp. 166-167
14. Ibid., p. 302

4. William Bramwell

1. James Sigston, *Memoir of the Life and Ministry of William Bramwell*, (New York: Eaton & Mains, 1820) p. 18
2. Rev. Thomas Harris, *Christian Minister in Earnest: A Portrait of the Rev. William Bramwell*, (London: Haymen, Christy & Lilly Ltd.) p. 16
3. Ibid., p. 24
4. Sigston, pp. 36-37
5. Harris, p. 25
6. Ibid., p. 40
7. Sigston, p. 65
8. Harris, p. 51
9. Ibid., p. 88
10. Ibid., pp. 92-93
11. Ibid., p. 112
12. Sigston, p. 206
13. Harris, p. 139
14. Ibid., p. 144
15. Ibid., p. 148
16. Ibid., p. 225
17. Ibid., p. 235
18. Ibid., p. 172
19. Ibid., p. 248
20. Ibid., p. 249
21. Ibid., p. 249

6. Felix Neff

1. Margaret AnneWyatt, translated by M. Bost, *Letters and Biography of Felix Neff* (London: R.B. Seeley & W. Burnside, 1843) p. 4
2. Ibid., p. 7
3. Ibid., p. 8
4. Ibid., p. 7
5. Ibid., p. 9
6. Ibid., pp. 9-10
7. Ernest B. Gordon, *A Book of Protestant Saints*, (Hampton: Harvey & Tait, 1991) pp.142-143
8. Wyatt, p. 29
9. Ibid., p. 33
10. Ibid., p. 39
11. Ibid., p. 36
12. Ibid., p. 49
13. Ibid., p. 62
14. Ibid., pp. 63-65
15. Ibid., pp. 69-70

16. Ibid., p. 86
17. Ibid., p. 88
18. Ibid., pp. 123-124
19. Ibid., pp. 143-146
20. Ibid., pp. 208-209
21. Ibid., pp. 301-302
22. Ibid., p. 337
23. Ibid., p. 386
24. Ibid., p. 167
25. Ibid., p. 125
26. Ibid., pp. 153-154
27. Ibid., p. 390

7. Robert Cleaver Chapman
1. Robert C. Chapman, *Hymns and Meditations*, (Glasgow: Pickering & Inglis) p. 75

9. Isaac Marsden
1. John Taylor, *Reminiscences of Isaac Marsden*, p. 22
2. Ibid., p. 72
3. Ibid., p. 39
4. Ibid., p. 51
5. Ibid., p. 53
6. Ibid., p. 55
7. Ibid., p. 67
8. Ibid., p. 159
9. Ibid., p. 183
10. Ibid., p.190
11. Ibid., p.179
12. Ibid., p.176
13. Ibid., p.181

10. Alfred Cookman
1. Henry B. Ridgaway, *The Life of Alfred Cookman*, (London: Hodder & Stoughton, 1875) p. 24
2. Ibid., p. 31
3. Ibid., p. 74
4. J. Olin Garrison, *Forty Witnesses*, pp. 239-241
5. Ibid., p. 241
6. Ridgaway, p. 125
7. Ibid., pp. 139-141

8. Ibid., pp. 156-157
9. Ibid., p. 289
10. Ibid., p. 294
11. Ibid., p. 296
12. Ibid., pp. 299-302
13. Ibid., p. 280

11. Elizabeth Baxter

1. Nathaniel Wiseman, *Elizabeth Baxter*, (London: The Christian Herald Co., Ltd., 1928) pp. 60-62
2. Ibid., p. 63
3. Ibid., p. 66
4. J. Olin Garrison, *Forty Witnesses*, pp. 277-278
5. Ibid., p. 278
6. Wiseman, p. 72
7. Garrison, p. 278
8. Wiseman, p. 85
9. Ibid., pp. 111-112
10. Ibid., p. 120
11. Ibid., p. 121
12. Ibid., p. 122
13. Garrison, p. 279
14. Wiseman, p. 134

12. Lilias Trotter

1. R. Govan Stewart, *The Love That Was Stronger*, (London: Lutterworth Press, 1958) pp. 14-15
2. Ibid., p. 22
3. Ibid., pp. 23-24
4. Lilias Trotter, *Smouldering*, pp. 6-8
5. Govan Stewart, p. 28
6. Ibid., p. 50
7. Ibid., p. 76
8. Constance E. Padwick, *The Master of the Impossible*, (London: Society for promoting Christian knowledge, 1938) p. 101

13. John Hyde

1. Canon R. H. A. Haslam, *Moody Monthly*, April 1945, p. 465
2. Francis A. McGraw, *Praying Hyde*, (Chicago: Moody Press) p. 11
3. Basil Miller, *Praying Hyde*, (Grand Rapids, Michigan: Zondervan Publishing House, 1943) p. 19

4. Ibid., pp. 40-41
5. Canon Haslam, p. 457
6. Miller, p. 130

14. Samuel Logan Brengle
1. Clarence Hall, *Samuel Logan Brengle*, (Chicago: The Salvation Army, 1933) pp. 47-48
2. Ibid., p. 52
3. Ibid., p. 72
4. Ibid., p. 102
5. Ibid., p. 105
6. Ibid., p. 87

15. Eva von Winkler
1. Sister Annie, *Sister Eva of Friedenshort*, (London: Hodder & Stoughton, 1934) pp. 37-38
2. Ibid., p. 38
3. Ibid., p. 40
4. Ibid., p. 42
5. Ibid., p. 93
6. Ibid., pp. 96-97
7. Ibid., p. 125
8. Ibid., pp. 127-128
9. Ibid., p. 129
10. Ibid., p. 130
11. Ibid., p. 131

17. Iva Vennard
1. Mary Ella Bowie, *Alabaster and Spikenard*, (Chicago: Evangelistic Institute, 1947) p. 46
2. Ibid., pp. 47-48
3. Ibid., p. 49
4. Ibid., p. 52
5. Ibid., p. 150
6. Ibid., p. 152
7. Ibid., p. 170
8. Ibid., pp. 180-181
9. Ibid., pp. 191-192
10. Ibid., p. 192
11. Ibid., pp. 196-197

They Knew Their God

VOLUME TWO

Gerhard Tersteegen (1697-1769) : Recluse in Demand
John Woolman (1720-1772) : Friend of the Oppressed
Elijah Hedding (1780-?) : The Pioneer Bishop
Robert Aitken (1800-1883) : Prophet of Pendeen
Mrs. Phoebe Palmer (1807-1872) : The Gift on God's Altar
Robert Murray McCheyne (1813-1843) : Youthful Saint of Dundee
William Burns (1815-1858) : The Man with the Book
Frances R. Havergal (1837-1879) : God's Songster
Pastor Hsi (1837-?) : Conqueror of Demons
George D. Watson (1845-1923) : Apostle to the Sanctified
Jessie Penn-Lewis (1861-1927) : Overcomer
The Three Garratt Sisters (late 1800's-mid 1900's) : The Three-fold Cord
Paget Wilkes (1871-1934) : Able Defender of the Faith
Basil Malof (1883-1957) : Apostle to Russia
Thomas Kelley (1893-1941) : Searcher and Finder
John and Betty Stam (?-1934) : Their Death was Gain
George Henry Lang (1874-1958) : God's Obedient Servant

They Knew Their God

VOLUME THREE

Marquis De Renty (1611 - 1649) : The Nobleman Who Stepped Down
Stephen Grellet (1773 - 1855) : French Nobleman on Foot
Samuel Pierce (1766 - 1799) : The Brainerd of the Baptists
John Smith (1794 - 1831) : The Man With Calloused Knees
Ann Cutler (1759 - 1794) : Too Young to Die
Uncle John Vassar (1813 - 1878) : God's Sheep Dog
George Railton (1849 - 1912) : The Man Who Cared Intensely
John G. Govan (1861 - 1927) : The Shepherd of Rural Evangelism
Oswald Chambers (1874 - 1917) : Apostle of the Haphazard
Gertrude Chambers (1885 - 1966) : Maker of Books
Evan Hopkins (1837 - 1919) : Messenger of Victory
Mary Mozley (1887 - 1923) : She Chose the Good Part
Francis Asbury (1745 - 1816) : The Fearless Itinerant

They Knew Their God

VOLUME FOUR

Phillip (1631 - 1696) and Matthew (1662 - 1714) Henry : The Making of a Commentator
Freeborn Garrettson (1752 - 1827) : Saint in the Saddle
Catherine Garrettson (1752 - 1849) : The Gracious Hostess
John Gossner (1773 - 1855) : Intrepid Adventurer in Faith and Prayer
John Hunt (1812 - 1848) : Apostle to Fiji
Elizabeth Prentiss (1818 - 1878) : The Suffering Succorer
Lord Radstock (1833 - 1913) : The Lord Who Served
Dr. Frederick Baedeker (1823 - ?) : A Man Sent from God
Frank Crossley (1839 - 1897) : God's Paymaster

They Knew Their God

VOLUME FIVE

George Herbert (1593 - 1632) : Poet of the Heavenly Court
Miguel Molinos (1627 - 1696) : The Priest Who Knew God
Joseph Alleine (1634 - 1668) : A Living Sacrifice at 34
John Fletcher (1729 - 1785) : Apostle of Madeley
Mary Fletcher (1739 - 1815) : Shepherdess of Orphans
Frederick Oberlin (1740 - 1826) : Pioneer Benefactor to the Vosges Dwellers
Samuel Pollard (1826 - 1877) : He Waited for the Fulfilment of His Vision
George Matheson (1842 - 1906) : The Blind Poet Who Saw Too Much
Jonathan Goforth (1859 - 1936) : He Suffered the Loss of All Things
Rosalind Goforth (1864 - ?) : She Climbed the Ascents With God
Kate Lee (1872 - 1920) : The Angel Adjutant
W. Graham Scroggie (1877 - 1954?) : The Unusual Keswick Speaker

They Knew Their God

VOLUME SIX

John Chrysostom (344-407) : The Fearless Bishop
John Brown (1722-1787) : The Cowherd Who Became Commentator
Charles Simeon (mid 1700's-1836) : A Man in Touch With God
Henry Martyn (1781-1812) : Too Young to Die?
Helen Ewan (early 1900's) : A Fragrant Life
Edward Payson (1783-1827) : He Discovered the Secret of Being Nothing
James Turner (1818-1862) : God's Fisherman
Thomas Waring (?) : The Silent Years
Anthony Norris Groves (1795-1853) : Pioneer in Apostolic Principles
Mary Bethia Groves (early 1800's) : The Once Reluctant Missionary
William Wilberforce (1759-1837) : A Rich Politician Called To Be God's Prophet
John Pierpont (early to mid 1800's) : God Compensates His Fearless Prophet
Johann Christoph Blumhardt (1805-1889) : The German Pastor Who Defied Devils
E. M. Bounds (1835-1913) : He Prayed While Others Slept